Personalisation for Socia

D0571312

3 (

Personalisation for Social Workers

OPPORTUNITIES AND CHALLENGES FOR FRONTLINE PRACTICE

Jenni Burton, Thomas Toscano and Maryam Zonouzi

Open University Press

Open University Press
McGraw-Hill Education
McGraw-Hill House
Shoppenhangers Road
Maidenhead
Berkshire
England
SL6 2QL

email: enquiries@openup.co.uk
world wide web: www.openup.co.uk

and Two Penn Plaza, New York, NY 10121-2289, USA

First published 2012

A catalogue record of this book is available from the British Library

ISBN-13: 978-0-33-524395-2 (pb)
ISBN-10: 0-33-524395-9 (pb)
eISBN: 978-0-33-524396-9

Library of Congress Cataloging-in-Publication Data
CIP data applied for

Typesetting and e-book compilations by
RefineCatch Limited, Bungay, Suffolk
Printed and bound in the UK by Bell & Bain Ltd, Glasgow

Fictitious names of companies, products, people, characters and/or data
that may be used herein (in case studies or in examples) are not intended
to represent any real individual, company, product or event.

The McGraw·Hill Companies

Contents

Introduction

This book is for both front line social work practitioners and for social work students as a practical guide to the unfolding transformation of adult social care services and the personalisation agenda. The structure of the book has been designed to encourage an interactive way of learning about personalisation as a fluid, ever changing and very important feature of modern day social work. Social workers have a key role to play in the reform of social care support and are at the heart of helping people to meet their individual needs. The book will reinforce the social work practitioner's role in the shaping of personalised support and will look broadly at the many influences on their role in order to gain a clearer understanding of contemporary issues, ethical dilemmas and tensions in practice.

Social work is essentially about helping and informing others to gain the support and resources needed to live their lives as fully as possible. The book will support students, qualifying students and front line workers to use essential skills such as communication, self reflection, creativity and empowerment to embrace the context of personalisation. This will be achieved by providing blended learning through the use of case studies, reflective exercises, linked research and reference to policies, legislation and resources to enable the reader to understand their role within the personalisation agenda.

The book will explore the topic of personalisation from many angles to consider how historical, political, financial and cultural influences have impacted upon the practical implementation of self directed support and the wide reaching impact for service users, families and both health and social care professionals. There will be an emphasis on current changes created by personalisation and also on where the initial ideas underpinning person centred approaches stemmed from. The book will also look ahead to the unfolding of personalisation and ongoing sustainability.

Finally, the book will focus on the need for the social work profession to embrace personalisation and to recognise the changes needed to ensure that social work practice can thrive and adapt to retain a central position as part of the personalisation environment.

Book structure

Chapter 1: Ethics, values and anti-oppressive practice

This chapter will focus on the values underpinning personalisation such as service user self determination, dignity and choice. Ethical dilemmas in social work practice will be explored to tease out the congruence between rights, responsibilities, duty to protect and the promotion of self directed support. Case studies and reflective learning will focus on the service user and carer perspectives and examples of personal, cultural and structural discrimination will be explored to reflect on the public understanding of personalisation. The chapter will also explore the intrinsic value base of social work and the changes needed to ensure that learning is gained through existing practice and developments.

Chapter 2: Social and political influences

This chapter will look at legislation and policy changes in social care implicit within personalisation spanning key legislation such as the Community Care, Mental Capacity and Human Rights Acts. The complex layering of social, political and ideological influences will be explored recognising the impact that personalisation has on our ideas of vulnerability, risk and citizenship. The emergence of policy with practice and the evolution of self directed support will be explored to gain a clearer view of where personalisation came from and what future shape may be to come.

Chapter 3: Opportunities and challenges in personalisation

The emphasis for this chapter will be on new ways of working with people who need social care support. There will be reflection on the dramatic changes for individuals and the impact on social work and social care. Good examples of practice will be highlighted and balanced with the challenges and the evolving role of the social work practitioner.

Chapter 4: Personalisation and safeguarding

This chapter will consider the risks attached to people living more independent lives as a result of self directed support and the role of social workers in safeguarding people who may be vulnerable to exploitation and abuse from others. The promotion of choice and control while reducing risk of harm will be explored through detailed analysis of case studies, reflective exercises and ideological debate. The impact of personalisation and safeguarding issues will be looked at from the perspectives of service users, families and professionals. Different theories, models and policies will be reflected on to capture emerging ideas and research on this diverse and complex aspect of the personalisation agenda.

Chapter 5: Experiences of personalisation from service users and carers

In this chapter we examine the diverse experiences of service users and carers who have personal support budgets. By drawing on a range of user centred case studies and the real experiences of individuals, the chapter will focus on the practicalities and some of the constraints of providing a personal budget and the role of the social worker in enabling service users to direct their own support. Different experiences and outcomes for individuals will be contrasted and the issues for families and carers will be included. Tensions will be explored in terms of the different experiences for individuals, how obstacles and challenges are experienced and how they can be overcome in practice.

Chapter 6: Dreams to reality: the way forward

This chapter will look at the changes that personalisation will bring to people and society and will examine the political and financial influences that interface with personalisation and the impact this has on the social work role. This book is being written during a time of rapid change to the way that personalisation is being delivered, which is shaped by government thinking and policy. The move from care management to self directed support is having a significant impact for front line social work and requires analysis of the future shape and function of social work practice. The chapter will focus on the changing arena of adult social care at an individual, local and national level to provide scope for practitioners to engage with some of the questions and uncertainties remaining in relation to the implementation and development of personalisation.

1

Ethics, values and anti-oppressive practice

Introduction

The intention of this chapter is to focus on the ethics and values which are central to personalisation and the impact for service users, carers and front line social work practitioners. Personalisation has a multi-layered framework of political, financial and cultural contexts which will be explored initially, in order to understand contemporary practice in adult social care more clearly and to identify the drivers which influence personalisation.

First it is important to clarify what we mean by values. Values are essentially a set of beliefs, ideas and assumptions that individuals and groups hold about themselves and their society. Ethical values indicate whether an action is 'right' or 'wrong'. Social work values and ethics are professional values enshrined within the professional code of practice and are centred on the importance of respecting the rights and needs of service users and carers and the importance of anti-oppressive practice. Personal values are those held by individuals and may be shared or kept as private and confidential. Personal and professional values may conflict or compete with each other and different people may prioritise different values, which can create the tensions and challenges within social work practice.

We will now briefly explore the broader framework of personalisation, as it is essential to recognise that personalisation is a concept spreading far beyond the remit of social work and can be seen as a 'whole system change' for health and social care.

The socio-political context driving the personalisation agenda emerged as a strong force under the Conservative government in the 1980s from the principles of the post-war welfare state and the arrival of care management and a dispersal of state controlled provision. The purchaser/provider mixed economy of care became a feature of the 1990 NHS and Community Care Act and encouraged a shift from the statutory to the private and independent sector (Davies 1999: 329). The Community Care (Direct Payments) Act 1996 was the first legislative move to shape the direction of personalised support and funding to meet individual needs. The Coalition Conservative/Liberal Government formed in 2011 has embraced the transformation of public services and the notion of the individual, the family and society taking increased responsibility for procuring and supporting their social care needs. Ferguson (2007) suggests that the evolution of personalisation has been driven by the government think tank rather than social work and argues that there are structural issues to be challenged in the process of devolving responsibility from the state to the individual, which may result in the transfer of increased control and autonomy to the service user but also brings with it the problems and challenges of limited resources and reduced eligibility to funding. It is therefore important to consider how personalisation has taken shape in the United Kingdom and how the concept can be seen to be 'Eurocentric' and more relevant to the modernisation of adult social care in westernised society, triggered by the prevailing demographic and financial pressures. We will be looking in more detail at some of these influences in the next chapter, which focuses on the social policy pertinent to personalisation.

Financial drivers have also been influential in the changing shape of the person-alisation agenda, as the need for transparency, clear and tightly budgeted outcomes and indicators across local authorities becomes paramount. The competition in the mixed economy of adult social care has created the idea of the service user as a 'consumer' of services and care as a commodity to be purchased. Barnett (2006) has argued that this is a difficult concept, as there may well be limited choice in terms of what services are on offer to purchase, and also the notion of rational choice for the consumer in social care terms may create a tension; 'consumers of health and social care may not possess the usual attributes of sound judgement and rationality that consumers are usually assumed to possess' (Le Grand et al. 2008: 55). Later in the chapter we will explore some of the tensions between the idea of the service user as a consumer of commodities and the principles of citizenship.

The social, cultural influences are also important to stress here, as is the philosophy of personalisation stemmed from person centred planning and the need to

> start with the individual as a person with strengths and preferences who may have a network of support and resources, which can include family and friends. They may have their own funding sources or be eligible for state funding. Personalisation reinforces the idea that the individual is best placed to know what they need and how these needs can be met . . . Personalisation is about giving people choice and control over their lives.
>
> (SCIE 2008/2010: 4)

The Valuing People legislation in 2001 really spearheaded the personalisation movement and also embraced the social model of disability, which recognises that it is the structure of society that creates the barriers for disabled people and that changes are needed to remove the obstacles that impede individuals from full inclusion within their community.

Personalisation can therefore be seen as a richly textured, complex and often contradictory concept, which promotes individual rights and equality, yet also carries the burden of financial and political constraints on personal funding and resources. Personalisation is therefore a 'value loaded' term, meaning different things to different people. The intention of the chapter is to cast some light on the contrasting views of service users, carers and practitioners and to explore some of the ethical dilemmas intrinsic to the transforming arena of adult social care.

Learning objectives for the chapter

1   To consider how personalisation has enabled service users to have a central place in the planning and delivery of their social care support

2   To reflect on how power differentials can cause discrimination experienced by service users at different levels: personally, culturally and structurally

3   To introduce theory and social work models to understand the value base of personalisation

4   To look at the shifting role for carers and ethical dilemmas that can be experienced by carers, service users and practitioners due to changing ways of working together

Social work values and the impact of personalisation for practitioners

The social work profession is experiencing dramatic changes as it travels forward to take on board the unfolding of the personalisation agenda and the national restructuring of social care services. Although social work has always been associated with value based practice it has also been 'chameleon like' in the way that the approach to supporting people has altered over the years. This has included radical social work in the 1970s (Langan and Lee 1989), social justice based models (Jordan 1990) and care management (DH 1990) as the prominent contemporary model of social work. Care management is the social work model which is being shaped and modelled by personalisation and currently undergoing rapid change, particularly in adult social work.

The new professional framework for social workers recommended by the Social Work Reform Board (DH 2010) aims to enhance the value base of the social work code of practice. The current social work value base comprises of five basic values of human dignity and worth, social justice, service to humanity, integrity and competence (BASW 2012) The new professional standards framework will set out the expectations of social workers at each stage of their career and will be used as the foundation to inform the design and implementation of education and training in the national career structure. The proposed framework is composed of nine core capabilities: professionalism; values and ethics; diversity; rights, justice and economic well-being; knowledge; critical reflection; intervention skills; context and organisations; and professional leadership. The values and ethics core element of the social work professional framework is particularly relevant to this chapter and can help to shape the direction needed for personalising support. The service user's voice is becoming more central to the social work process and, as suggested by Manthorpe et al. (2008: 3), 'the process of personalisation will inevitably alter the world of social work and care management with adults'.

Reflective Exercise 1.1

As social work students or practitioners, we need to recognise our personal values and beliefs, which are of central importance in our lives and also be able to comply and fully practise professional ethics and values. When considering personalised support for service users and carers we need to be in tune with the values and beliefs of each person to ensure that the support provided is meaningful and carried out in the way that will be most helpful and empowering.

Thinking about your own personal values, make a list of those values you feel are important for living a quality lifestyle. How might you feel if others were to question your personal values and priorities? When reflecting on what gives value to our lives, quite strong feelings can be generated, particularly when our fundamental beliefs are challenged. This really shows the essential importance of our values as part of our individual identity and how we are able to live and experience a sense of well-being.

Personalisation can evoke quite diverse and emotive feelings and beliefs from people: the following two quotes are from two social work professionals who hold very different perceptions of personalisation. The opposing views reinforce the strength of opinion that the personalisation movement has triggered.

> Personalisation has little to do with caring and a lot to do with the presentation of political and economic programmes in the pursuit of government survival and re-election . . . the reality is in part an attempt to persuade the electorate that their shared vision and commitment to the transformation of adult social care through personalisation is worth voting for.
>
> (Burton 2010: 303)

> Personalisation does not mean care management by another name, but a systematic review of all existing procedures, business processes and practices, a shift from traditional care solutions involving service users and carers, capacity building in the 3rd sector, involving and communicating with social workers, creativity, trying new solutions and being prepared to be challenged.
>
> (Cleary 2010)

Reflective exercise 1.2

As a social work or social care practitioner there may well be elements of both quotes which chime with the changes happening as part of the transformation of adult services. This could include the restructuring of services, concerns about the quality of personal support due to financial cuts, pressure on voluntary provision to develop without adequate funds and support and the changes to the social work role itself. However, it could also be much more about examples of the positive impact of a personal budget for a service user you have worked with and the benefits gained or creative ways that different professionals are now working together to achieve clearer outcomes for individuals.

Now consider both the positive and negative influences of personalisation on your specific role or experiences and make a list of these; it may be interesting to reflect on any changes to your thinking as you continue reading this text!

Between these two starkly contrasting quotes and their different underpinning values are numerous different experiences and views, some of which we will consider throughout the chapter.

Reflective exercise 1.3

Our personal and professional values and beliefs are shaped and influenced in many different ways; by our family, friends, the media, our experiences during work and training courses and from our local community. Public perceptions of personalisation are influenced by the views of individuals and, conversely individual perspectives are shaped by the messages conveyed by the media in all its many guises. Consider the many ways that we gain information about personalisation; where we tend to gain the positive perspectives and where the more negative views tend to be presented. What are the factors that lead to the positive and negative views presented?

You may have come up with personal stories from individuals themselves explaining the ways that individual budgets have had a direct impact on their lives, coverage in journal articles about new projects or initiatives such as agencies offering support brokerage, or perhaps from political debates in newspapers considering government cuts and threats to individual budgets, etc.

Our ethics and values around personalisation and individuals eligible for this support are also informed by a wide range of influences which are multi-layered and can be reinforced by public perspectives.

The ways that public perceptions about personalisation are shaped can be understood and explored by referring to Thompson's seminal work on anti-oppressive practice and ingrained ideas within society about discrimination and inequality. Cultural ideology transmits powerful messages which become shared values and beliefs within society. A widely held idea within society, and perhaps influenced by the prevalence of the welfare state, considers how adults who are vulnerable in some way may be eligible for social care support and may therefore be perceived as 'needy' and dependent on the support of others. Thompson (1993) wrote about anti-discriminatory practice and a model known as the 'PCS' model which demonstrates how the ideas we hold about difference and discrimination stem from different levels of influence within our society. Discrimination and oppressive practice can evolve from shared ideas about people who are vulnerable and therefore may not be in a position of power or able to aspire to achieve a high status within society. In the PCS model Thompson refers to the 'P' level as the central point where influences can come from personal prejudice and language about a person who is different in some way perhaps due to age, race, class or disability. The 'C' level refers to the impact from society and the ways that public services and facilities can exclude individuals and groups due to barriers such as limited access, limits on employability, restrictions on choices due to cultural preferences, etc. The final layer, 'S', is the overarching structural ideology which sets the financial, political and legal framework around the personal and cultural layers, and has implicit and explicit 'rules' about status and achievements which are highly prized in society and can be hard to attain for individuals who are vulnerable in some way due to age, disability or other differences.

The PCS model helps to recognise how we all gather and internalise ideas about the services and support people need and how a personal approach to support may help to break down the differences which can separate adults into needing separate and exclusive services.

Personalisation as a government led initiative within adult social care appears to be primarily familiar to those individuals and their families eligible for personal funding and support who will then have direct knowledge about the role of social work and other linked professions. This can be contrasted with the broader knowledge held by health and social care professional journals and websites which are able to promote the positive messages of personalisation directly expressed by recipients themselves.

The service user and carer perspective

As mentioned in Thompson's PCS model, there are structural factors within society that are instrumental to creating inequality and oppression which has been deep rooted for hundreds of years. There is a rich history spanning the eighteenth, nineteenth and twentieth centuries of people who have become vulnerable due to misfortune, poverty, illness, age or disability becoming separated from their families and communities to live in institutional care: 'People who were mentally ill, disabled, old or even just "socially unacceptable" like some unmarried mothers, were forced to live in large, congregated and segregated camps with lives characterised by tedium, diminished status, deprivation and systematic abuse' (Jones 1993). Social work has always been targeted towards the sector of society which is marginalised in some way due to poverty, disability or vulnerability, rather than being openly available to all society as is the case in public sector services such as education and health. (Beresford and Croft 2001).

The shifting power dynamics central to personalised support and funding will be illustrated by looking first at a service user perspective and then considering the impact of personalisation for a carer who has become eligible for social care support and her mother, to compare and contrast their experiences and examine how both of their lives have become affected by the dramatic changes brought about by the transformation of adult social care.

The first case study looks at the changes for a young woman with learning disabilities who has experienced both traditional mainstream support and also more recently, self directed funding and support.

CASE STUDY 1.1

Ellie is a young woman, aged 22, with moderate learning disabilities and an autistic spectrum condition. Ellie is able to manage her own personal care needs and is able to communicate with others although her speech is limited to very short sentences. At times the pressure of communicating and being with other people in different social situations can be overwhelming and Ellie can become withdrawn and depressed. Ellie lives at home with her parents, a 10-year-old brother and an older sister, aged 24, who has recently had a baby. The house is very noisy and quite crowded as parents, three siblings, the older daughter's partner and the baby all live together in the semi-detached house with three bedrooms. The added dimension of the baby in the family home has had a dramatic effect on Ellie, who is experiencing delayed puberty and has become very fixated on the baby. There have been incidents when Ellie has taken the baby from her cot at night and tried to nurse her. Ellie shared a bedroom with her brother which has caused friction and has created a difficult relationship between them.

Ellie attends a local day service for three days of the week and a college course for one further day. Due to the tensions within the family dynamics and some concerns raised about Ellie's increasingly withdrawn behaviour at the day service, a social worker has carried out a home visit to assess the situation. Following a review of the initial Community Care Assessment completed three years ago when Ellie left children's services, the suggestion of supported living and a personal support budget is made to Ellie and her parents. A self referral is completed, a resource allocation request put in place and a support plan for personal support is implemented.

Ellie begins a transition plan to gradually move into her own flat near to the family home. Her older sister is part of the support plan and has agreed to spend two hours every day helping Ellie to settle into her new home. Ellie also has a personal assistant to support her with daily living support. Part of her personal budget will also pay for Ellie to increase her college attendance to two days a week although her day service place will be phased out, due to the ongoing closure of day services as part of the local authority restructuring.

One year on, Ellie has started to enjoy her independence. This was a slow process and family involvement began to compromise her confidence in making decisions for herself. A review involving Ellie, family members, the social worker and the personal assistant identified a plan of action to clarify where Ellie needed the support to be targeted. She now has a part time job at a local garden centre and attends a college course to complete a horticulture qualification. Ellie now shares a flat with another disabled woman and has had her personal support hours reduced from 30 to 20 hours each week. The support is tailored to her particular needs for help with budgeting, food shopping and daily living skills such as use of public transport. Ellie is beginning to make a contribution to her community through her job and also her interest in a local conservation group which meets every week.

Questions to consider

Ellie is experiencing many changes in her life at a time of transition from being a young person to becoming an adult with her own home and increased independence.

1   What are some of the issues that Ellie will need to adjust to as part of the process of change?

2   In what ways will Ellie experience more choice and control about how she lives?

3   What support will Ellie need to have to ensure that she is able to manage the balance between having both increased access to rights and also new responsibilities ?

4   In what ways can Ellie begin to contribute to her local community and be accepted as a citizen with valued skills and qualities to offer to others?

Issues arising

There are some key issues which arise from the case study and the questions considered. Reflective learning and thinking provides a vital tool for social work students and practitioners to explore more deeply the impact of life experiences for service users and to ensure that practice is ethical and is based on 'values-in-action'. Bolton (2010) writes about the central importance of the relationship between the service user and the social worker and the ethical principles of reflective practice:

> Trust in our own personal insight . . . Self-respect for our beliefs, actions, feelings, values and identity . . . Responsibility for our own actions . . . Generosity of our energy, time and commitment and Positive Regard in the way we understand how and why things have happened.
>
> (Bolton 2010: 47–48)

We will now consider some of the issues arising from the case study and link these to theories, research and social work methods to help us to 'unpack' some of the personal experiences for Ellie and relate these more broadly to the ethics and values intrinsic to personalised support for vulnerable adults.

Transition and change

Ellie is embarking on a journey of fast and significant change in many aspects of her life. The central ethos of personalisation is to ensure that changes are planned in a way that ensures that the person and their family are kept fully involved and central to any changes. The mantra for 'Valuing People' (2001 and 2009b) 'Nothing About Us Without Us' has become of vital importance to the personalisation process. How can personalised budget support be introduced gradually and with sensitivity to avoid anxiety and to ensure that the person feels in control of the changes happening in their life?

You may have reflected on the impact that dramatic change would have on anyone moving from their family home, their day time occupation and from the friends and contacts established on a daily basis. Ellie may find these changes even more unsettling due to her particular communication needs, her tendency to withdraw from unplanned changes to her routines and her attachments to her sister's baby, as well as the familiarity with a service and people she has known for several years. Individualising the support plan for Ellie and breaking the changes down to specific stages, gradually reducing the time spent at the day service and introducing independent living skills at the right pace for Ellie will enable her to feel in control of the process. Also ensuring that Ellie has informed choices and can try out new opportunities before committing to them, and that important family members are involved in her support plan are some of the ways to ensure that the support is personalised.

When considering the transition from traditional to self directed support for learning disabled adults it is clear that there will be losses as well as gains, as adjustments are made from group care models of support to independent living. Public perceptions of learning disabled people commonly hold deep rooted ideas about the dependence of disabled people on others and the inability to fully participate as citizens within society. David Sibley wrote about marginalised groups within communities in his text *Geographies of Exclusion* (1997). Sibley reflects on the boundaries created within special environments to segregate groups of people who are seen to be different in some way: 'who is felt to belong and not to belong contributes in an important way to the shaping of social space' (Sibley 1997: 4).

Day services have their place in history, and can be seen to be part of the time line of segregated services starting with asylums and moving forward to hospitals and large institutions, which later transformed into residential and day services in the 1960s. Although the quality of the segregated service model has improved over the years, there remains an ingrained expectation from some sectors of society that vulnerable adults will be separated, supported and protected from the full risks of ordinary life. Ellie, like thousands of other disabled people moving from day services across the country as part of the transformation of adult social care, will have developed many important relationships with other disabled people and may have established a sense of belonging and self assurance within a service setting geared to supporting people with their particular needs. Personalisation is not a 'quick fix' for young disabled people like Ellie, who may feel vulnerable in the move from a familiar environment to the unknown experience of the freedom of a home of her own. The personalised approach will take time to develop to ensure that Ellie remains central to the changes and is supported in a sensitive and creative way to access the new opportunities available to her.

A relevant methodology for social work intervention with adults is the 'systems approach', which is a way of developing a holistic view of the life experiences of the individual and providing a focus for service users' lives that may easily be missed or glossed over. By looking at Ellie's life and all the people and influences that are important to her it is possible to also look more broadly at the 'fit' between people and their social environments. We will go on to look at power differentials and the way that power is distributed in networks and communities, and how much power is actually held by individuals being supported within them.

Power differentials

Smale et al. (2000) has written about the power held within communities and the power dynamics between individuals, groups and communities:

> Many people are in communities which ignore, neglect, reject or persecute them or in some way cause them stress or leave them alone with their pain. Most people

are in communities and networks where resources are unevenly distributed and some feel powerless relative to others. Often people known to workers are in networks that label them as 'clients'. The workers will deliberately or unwittingly but nevertheless inevitably be part of these processes.

(Smale et al. 2000: 90, cited in Smith)

It is this shift in mindset from unwittingly colluding with the traditional, paternalistic division between the professional worker and the client that personalisation seeks to dissolve.

Reflecting on the dramatic changes Ellie will start to experience as part of the transformation of adult services, a significant influence will be the power differentials at play, which Ellie will gradually adjust to. Personalisation is an approach which seeks to enable individuals to gain more control and choice over their life and therefore to be empowered to make new decisions and increase the quality of their life. Power differentials refer here to the move away from traditional, more dependent forms of care towards a more equitable relationship with social care practitioners, carers and local agencies. Adams et al. (2008) identified a framework for service users to determine different power strategies. These can be seen as a sliding scale of power differentials:

- compliance
- non-cooperation
- resistance
- challenge
- collaboration
- control

(Adams et al. 2008: 126)

Ellie could be seen to be moving slowly forward from a compliant position of power, unable to elicit a great deal of influence on her life either at home or within a busy group setting of a day service. The provision of a personal support plan should enable her to move towards recognising her dissatisfaction with aspects of her life and to be able to challenge the changing dynamics of the family unit. The move towards collaboration and the transition plan centred on Ellie's needs and interests could be seen to be moving towards the direction of equalising the power balance between service users, carers and professionals. This is a fairly generalised idea of power differences between service users and others who have an impact in their lives but it does provide an interesting overview of how incremental changes can interplay to create a model of support which will gradually provide more independence and choice to Ellie in the ways she may decide to manage her life.

The ultimate strategy of power linked to the ethos of personalisation would be to enable service users to exercise complete control over the way in which needs are defined, rights are recognised and interventions are determined. Oliver links this to the way that disability is defined by culture: 'crucial to this consideration is the

distinction between organisations *for* the disabled and organisations *of* disabled people'
(Oliver 1990: 113).

The notion of deconstructing power differentials and developing power sharing
approaches with a more radical model of partnership working between service users,
carers and practitioners is at the heart of personalisation. Rogowski has written about
the central importance of the relationship between the paid worker and the service
user. Certainly, personal assistants will be intimately involved in individual's lives as
part of the support plan, although it is vital to retain a professional and personal divide
to ensure that blurred boundaries are not created. Personalised support treads a fine
line between recognising that there is a power imbalance in professional–user
relationships, yet that the relationship needs to be person centred and ensure that the
power is transferred to the service user in relation to the process of self assessment,
support planning and allocation of the budget. When exploring the statutory aspects of
the social work role it is clear that there are tasks which need to be carried out to
gate keep and protect the service user and the resources available to them. The task of
assessment, resource allocation and monitoring the budget remain vital parts of the
personalised support carried out by social workers and social care staff. The partnership
between social workers and service users is based on the citizenship model which we will
go on to explore.

Citizenship

Perhaps as important as the power differentials for Ellie making the transition from
attending a segregated day service and living at home will be the opportunity to live
as an ordinary citizen in her own home and to be able to choose which mainstream
services she can access.

Reflective exercise 1.4

At the beginning of the chapter the notion of the service user as a consumer of social
care services was raised. We will now pause to consider what ideas we associate with
being a consumer as compared to being a citizen. Think for a moment about the
differences in both terms and come up with a list of characteristics for consumerism
and for citizenship.

Your understanding of consumerism may well be linked with the service user as a
recipient of social care, which is purchased as an economic transaction. This is
certainly part of the personalisation process and links the individual with schemes
such as direct payments and individual budgets which are available in the 'market'.
The transformation of the adult social care 'market' has created more choice and
diversity for service users but has also introduced measures of increased rationing of
funding tightly controlled by assessment of eligibility for support. The service user as
a consumer is a definition which seems to emphasise the economic approach to
concepts of choice and control and can create an environment of increased risk for
individuals who may not have capacity to understand what choices are in their best

interest and may be at risk of increased harm. Madelstam (2009) suggests that the increased risk to the individual within the context of a consumerist approach to social care may be linked to safeguarding issues.

Citizenship is a term which suggests much broader ideas about the individual as being socially included in society, being able to exercise their rights and being free to have choice and control about their own lives. There is a tension between the concept of consumerism and citizenship which can be minimised by addressing the anti-oppressive value of the citizenship model as part of the ethos of personalisation. Citizenship is linked closely with personalisation and should provide the trigger for service users to practise their individual rights to live as equal to all adults within society:

> Social work is a practical profession, aimed at helping people address their prob-
> lems and matching them with resources they need to lead healthy and productive
> lives. Beneath this practicality lies a strong value system that can be summarised
> in two words; Social Justice.
>
> (Duffy 2006)

Simon Duffy has researched the topic of personalisation to develop a theory and practice base centred on the notion of 'Citizenship Theory'. Duffy is the Director of the Centre for Welfare Reform and an avid contributor to the understanding of personalisation. His quote crystallises the importance he places on the service user as a citizen within society: 'The drive to self directed support comes from the recognition that society has often failed those who need support by providing it in ways that limit and constrain the individual. Too often the price of receiving support is exclusion from the life of citizenship' (Duffy et al. 2010: 257).

Duffy's Citizenship Theory is central to the ethos of personalisation because it promotes the message that every person in society is of equal worth and is equal in dignity, seeing human difference as a positive attribute. Duffy has identified the 'keys to citizenship' as:

- autonomy
- direction
- money
- home
- support
- contribution

Duffy's work on citizenship as a central core of personalisation builds on Wolfensberger's important work on 'Normalisation' and 'Social Role Valorisation', which became well established during 1960s and 1970s. Wolfensberger's emphasis on the importance of supporting people to play socially valued roles as citizens had significant influence in shaping current ideas about person centred support. The sense of a progression of ideas through time linked by the value base of personalised approaches is an aspect to reflect on as we move on to consider the impact of personalised support on those family carers who are important people in the lives of the service users receiving personal support through individual budgets.

Co-production and partnership working

In the case study Ellie is able to work part time and become involved in local volunteering in her community. By taking on roles in society which are valued by others as part of being a citizen Ellie is able to fully participate and enjoy an inclusive lifestyle. Personalisation recognises the need for service users and carers to be involved at every stage of support planning from self assessment through to implementation and evaluation. Co-production is a term referred to in the Government White Paper *Putting People First* (DH 2007) which is concerned with looking in a positive way at the contributions that individuals, their families and practitioners can make to their own lives and the lives of others in their community. This creates a shift from paternalistic dependency on the state as the provider for those seen to be vulnerable within society.

We will now move on to consider the family carer and their important role as part of the personalisation process.

CASE STUDY 1.2

Charlene is the daughter of Hilda, who is 85 years old and has increasing physical health issues, including a stroke and diabetes and both sight and hearing impairments. Charlene is a training consultant for a large company and has been promoted to establish a new site located several hundred miles away. As the main carer and a single mother with two grown up sons living away from home, Charlene moves home with her mother to take up the promotion opportunity. Charlene contacts the nearest social work department to arrange for her mother to be assessed for support. Hilda is assessed as eligible for a personal budget as her needs are within the critical need band (Fair Access to Care, 2003, Dept of Health). Charlene is the main carer during the evening and weekend hours and therefore only requests personal support for her mother during the weekdays. Hilda is allocated a total of 20 hours a week support from a personal assistant. This provides a supportive environment for Hilda who now has help with washing, dressing, assistance with meals and support to enable her to visit the local lunch and leisure club in the next village. Hilda starts to make new friends and enjoy a sense of a more individualised pattern to her life. The personal support contrasts with her previous support before having the personal budget, which was very limited and based mainly on three mornings a week at a Red Cross day centre located 15 miles from home.

Charlene however, is finding the balance between her new demanding work role, adjusting to a new home and environment and caring for her mother when not at work very challenging. Recently the personal assistant has become unreliable and there have been concerns about items going missing from the house. Charlene has had to seek advice from the social work team and to employ another personal carer for her mother. Hilda's needs are increasing and the responsibility of managing the financial monitoring of the personal budget falls on Charlene. Charlene becomes depressed and often finds the role of being the main carer overwhelming.

Questions to consider

1   What are some of the challenges for Charlene as the main carer for Hilda?
2   What changes has Hilda experienced since receiving personal budget support?

Issues arising

Charlene is one of thousands of women in this country who are unpaid carers. The majority of working age carers, especially those providing care for 20 hours or more each week, are female (Maher and Green 2002). Also, the demand for labour has resulted in a situation where women in their 40s and 50s are being targeted by employers and the government to remain in the workplace (Department of Work and Pensions 2005). This is happening at the same time as more care demands are falling on women (and men) as the possibility of taking on the caring role increases with age. In Britain, the peak age for starting a caring role is between 45 and 64 years. (Hirst 2000).

As reflected in this case study the personalisation of support can create tensions for the carer, which are complex and need a sensitive and creative response to enable the carer to feel emotionally supported to cope.

There is certainly a delicate balance between achieving the right level and kind of support for the service user and the carer and also the overarching constraints and discrepancies between what is needed and what can be funded. Charlene has targeted the support for her mother during week days when she is working and manages all the care support herself during the evenings and weekends. This may put a strain on her quality of life and be difficult to sustain in the longer term.

Hilda has been able to have an assessment of her needs which has identified some personalised support and access to services which were not available to her before the move. The interdependency of the service user and the carer can be seen to be essential to ensure that the personal support plan can be maintained.

Peter Beresford, long term mental health service user and campaigner for the rights of service users and carers, considers the disparities between what individuals and families receive due to tightening eligibility bands: 'It's not difficult to understand service user's and carer's rising concerns. Eligibility criteria have undoubtedly tightened and personal budget cash ceilings are falling in the wake of unprecedented public spending cuts' (Beresford 2011).

The two case studies have explored some of the benefits and also some of the tensions within personal models of support. The complexity of personalisation is partly due to the challenge of responding to individual needs, wants and aspirations while also complying with the ethics and values implicit within the social work profession. The final section of the chapter will consider some of the ethical dilemmas in practice, which require sensitive and skilled responses from practitioners.

Ethical dilemmas in practice

Personalisation could be argued to be the most dramatic force to impact on the social work profession in the adult support sector since community care legislation was introduced in the 1990s. Social work practitioners are experiencing significant changes in the re-shaping of organisations to accommodate the move to personal assessments and support planning. At the same time many local authorities and private, voluntary and independent services are targeting reduced budgets to ensure that the support is at the right level for individual service users and carers. This has in some areas resulted in a reduction in social work jobs and an increase in new posts such as support brokers. There are also fears that personalisation is being directly affected by budget cuts which are leading to reduced choice and control. Jon Glasby, co-author of *Direct Payments and Personal Budgets* (Glasby and Littlechild 2009) has expressed his concerns about the challenges faced by adult social care, stating that social workers felt 'isolated and alienated – as if personalisation is giving them empowering language but that it is being set up to fail by a financial context that makes it impossible to deliver' (Community Care 10th February 2011).

Reflective exercise 1.5

The impact of personalisation for the social work profession is significant; the service users funded by local authorities are becoming the purchasers of their support through their personal budgets. This alters the working relationship between the service user, carer and the professional provider of the support required. There is an interesting comparison to be made between social workers before personalisation, as generic providers of assessed services, with that of the traditional model of a large supermarket providing the customer a whole array of goods which can be purchased by them from one main location. This is slowly changing to a more personalised service where produce can be selected by the customer in their own home and delivered to their door to offer a tailor-made service. In a similar way social workers now need to adapt to individualised ways of working which are flexible to the needs of the customers.

What are some of the advantages to this change in the provision of social work support to the individual social worker?

There are several benefits that spring to mind, such as the opportunity to work in a closer and more responsive way with service users and carers. With the emphasis on value for money, social workers can enable service users and carers to source local services and support by developing their knowledge of the community resources. The move away from separate services for service users can generate scope for social workers to be more creative in finding ways of enabling people to live in the community with their families and friends. There are also the benefits of increased inter-professional working and ability for social workers to work more widely with other professionals and local services thus valuing expertise and working together for the benefit of all. Of course, personalisation will not be an easy journey for the social work profession and will introduce many challenges to values and pose many ethical dilemmas along the way!

Social work is shifting to accommodate the altered direction of how eligible adults are being supported and the picture is still uncertain as to exactly how they will fit in to the overall framework of support needed. Certainly, there are opportunities for creative and community based working which is true to traditional social work values; however there will be many practical dilemmas without easy solutions! Financial restrictions placed upon personalisation have triggered social workers and social work academics to reflect on the pervading bureaucracy within social work and raise concerns about the tension between building relationships with individuals and providing a service. 'Relationship based work is at the heart of good social work practice, simply because all social work begins and ends with a human encounter' (Rogowski 2010: 24). Rogowski views the managerial nature of care management approaches to social work as counterproductive to the central concern of building relationships with service users and carers, sustaining them and ending them. These tensions within contemporary social work are complex and difficult to unravel. As a way of reflecting on the value base of personalised ways of working in practice, this section of the chapter will focus on three ethical dilemmas.

1 Professional and personal boundaries

CASE STUDY 1.3

Elliot is a newly qualified social worker based in a multi-professional community team for people with mental health needs. He is working with a CPN (community psychiatric nurse) to support a young man who has moved on from hospital discharge and subsequent supported housing to his own house in the town. The young man, Harry, is 26 and has a bi-polar disorder and severe damage to his lower spine, both due to a serious motor bike accident two years ago. Harry now has outreach support from the CPN, and Elliot has been allocated to monitor the direct payment. This was set up six months previously by a colleague in the social work team and a personal assistant was employed by Harry for three mornings a week. Before making an appointment to meet Harry at home to review the support plan in place, he reads the information on file. A contact report from another social worker in the team states: 'I was surprised to note on my first home visit following the employment of the personal assistant that Harry seemed very subdued and reluctant to comment on how things were progressing. The flat was very clean and tidy and all seemed to be in order.' When Elliot visits he is greeted by the personal assistant at the door. She is a woman called Rebecca who is in her early 30s. Harry seems relaxed and happy and is able to explain how his support plan is being met and where the help is most needed.

Elliot is relieved that all seems fine, the support hours seem to be adequate for Harry, the budget is being managed and records are up to date. Just before Elliot leaves he hears Rebecca ask Harry if she can borrow £5 until tomorrow. He is very reluctant to create any difficulties as all is going so well and leaves without comment.

Questions to consider

1   Elliot has been given information from a social work colleague about the service user. How should Elliot make a distinction between what is 'factual' information in the case file and what is 'opinion' formed by judgement? How may this differ from his own perception of the situation when he visits the service user at home?

2   As a newly qualified social worker Elliot will need to be able to both 'reflect in action' during the home visit and 'reflect on action' after the intervention with the service user (Schön 1983). In what ways could Elliot assess the situation and respond to the conversation he witnessed both immediately at the time of the visit and then later?

3   Elliot will need to consider the professional and personal boundaries around the service user as an employer and the personal assistant as his employee. What risks may there be to both Harry and Rebecca if clear protocols are not in place? How should Elliot ensure that he adheres to the professional social work code of practice?

Linked research

Healy and Mulholland (2007: 14) state: 'You should always try to represent yourself in your writing as thoughtful, objective, experienced and careful about what you communicate.' The ethical value base of writing as a social worker is as important as both verbal and non verbal forms of communication. Elliot may find this a useful learning point to ensure that he is clear about how recorded information needs to be presented and also how to respond to this when he meets the service user and makes his own judgement based on factual information and his views of what is happening. Elliot has the dilemma of deciding how to respond straight away to what he observes and then deciding what to do with the information after he leaves the service user's home. The process of decision making needs to be shaped by values, anti-discriminatory practice and the ethic of empowering service users and carers. This needs to be balanced with the need to ensure that the statutory duty of professional social work is upheld. If there is evidence that public funds are being displaced and there is a risk of financial abuse, even if it seems a small amount of money, this does need to be reported and investigated. Elliot will need to ensure that Harry is fully involved in this process to ensure that a person centred rather than paternalistic perspective is practised so that Harry's own capacity to make decisions is not undermined. Support from Elliot's line manager will also be important for his ongoing personal and professional development.

2 Assessing risk

CASE STUDY 1.4

Gloria is 83 years old and lives with her husband Eric in their own bungalow. They have been married for 50 years and want to remain together. Gloria has been diagnosed with dementia and has recently become very unsettled and unsure of where she is and tends to lash out at Eric. Eric, who is 78 years old, is struggling to cope although he has diabetes and is becoming quite frail and tired. Both receive meals on wheels and domiciliary care each day which are paid for as part of their direct payment from the local authority. The house is becoming difficult to manage and they restrict use to one room, which is used as a bedroom and living space. Eric collects war memorabilia and any available space is used to store his collection. The social worker allocated to both Gloria and Eric is called Carrie. She has recently visited to do a self assessment and carer's assessment to monitor the personal budget allocated and managed by the team for older people. The other reason for the visit was to respond to several complaints from neighbours about screaming and loud crying noises from the house. During the visit Carrie notices that Gloria has several bruises on her upper arms and seems very confused and unwell. Eric discloses that he has to use force to get Gloria to get up from the chair and into bed which has caused the bruising. Carrie observes that they both look to each other for comfort and are very warm and caring to each other. Both Gloria and Eric are desperate to remain at home and are very happy with the support they already receive from home care, meals on wheels and the district nurse who monitors Eric's diabetes and Gloria's dementia. Carrie has to decide either to leave the situation as it is or assess the risks as too high for Gloria and Eric to remain at home together.

Questions to consider

1   How can Carrie balance her need to keep the couple safe with their personal wish to remain at home together? What assessments will she need to complete in order to help her gather together the information required?

2   Carrie is expected to work in a person centred way to ensure that both Gloria and Eric's needs and aspirations are considered. What risk enablement skills will help to progress the assessment?

3   Carrie is dealing with a complex and sensitive situation. What social work skills will enable her to look at the issues from different perspectives and ensure that intervention is objective, creative and based on social work values, rather than responding directly to policies and procedures?

Linked research

Carrie will be assessing the risks to both Gloria and Eric in terms of their future life together at home. Titterton (2005) refers to different types of risk assessments and promotes positive risk taking. This involves weighing up the potential benefits and harms of exercising one choice of action over another, being clear about the risk, and setting out plans and actions which reflect the positive capabilities and the stated priorities from the service user and carer perspectives. Gaylard (2009: 63) identifies different variables to take into consideration when prioritising risk:

- physical capability of the user;
- mental capacity of the user;
- environment; is it safe for both the user and carer?
- actions already taken to reduce risk.

Carrie will also need to use her skills of reflection and critical analysis to ensure that she is able to think creatively about the many factors and the best interests of both Gloria and Eric. Gillie Bolton has written widely about reflective practice and the importance of 'through the mirror' writing and 'opening up to close observation uncertainty' and questioning previously taken for granted areas such as;

- Actions; what you and others did
- Ideas; what you thought and what others might have thought
- Feelings; what you felt and what others might have felt.

(Bolton 2010: 33)

3 Citizenship and diversity

> **CASE STUDY 1.5**
>
> Rita is a 37-year-old second generation Asian woman. Rita has learning disabilities and has had a long term gastric complication since her adolescence, which has now resulted in terminal stomach cancer. Rita lives in a very close and protected environment with her elderly parents and two sisters. Rita has experienced minimal rights, choice and freedom to live independently due to the cultural beliefs of the father and the perceived 'double discrimination' experienced due to being a disabled woman within a traditional Asian family household. The local health centre has passed on concerns to the social work team about poor health and hygiene within the family and a diet that is heavily based on fried foods and processed ready meals. The family doctor assessed this to be a probable factor in the stomach problems Rita has experienced over the years. Her family have not allowed her to attend a local day service and she has lived at home since leaving school, although she is chaperoned by her parents to a multi-cultural centre two mornings a week. Rita is now being cared for in hospital and it is expected that she will have just a few weeks to live.
>
> Both Rita and her family wish her to return home for her end of life care. She is particularly close to one of her sisters who provides the personal care she requires and is paid a direct payment to enable Rita to be looked after at home.

Rita has mental capacity to decide what happens. The social worker allocated to the case, Sarah, wants to support Rita and her family but is concerned that Rita will not receive the best medical care and support if she is moved and may not be able to have the dignity and the rights she is entitled to when at home. The hospital staff feel that minimal medical care can now be offered and any day to day nursing will be managed by the trained community nurses.

Questions to consider

1 What are the main factors that Sarah will need to consider before making a decision?

2 How can Sarah begin to discover what Rita would prefer to happen to her as the end of life plan?

3 What will be particularly important skills for Sarah to demonstrate both to Rita, to the family and to other professionals?

4 What are some of the tensions within this scenario, which are heightened by the issues of cultural and religious differences and which need to be considered?

Linked research

Personalisation needs to encompass the personal support and help given to a vulnerable person right through to the end of their life. Sarah will have many factors to weigh up and consider including the most helpful way to communicate with Rita to find out her views. Rita may prefer to use photographs, pictures or signing as preferred ways of expressing her views (Koprowska 2010).

Sarah will need to work closely with other professionals to ensure that decisions are taken with all the information available and ensure that liaison with the family is carried out in a united and collaborative way. The family will also be experiencing loss and grief and will have their own cultural and religious beliefs which need to be respected. There may be family expectations of taking on the caring role (A Lifetime of Caring 2005) and important records of the person's life to be maintained such as memories, family tree, photographs and valued possessions. This needs to be balanced with Rita's right to a high standard of palliative care at the end of life (Blackman and Todd 2005).

Chapter summary

The ethical dilemmas social workers may encounter on a daily basis are often due to the need to balance confidentiality with the duty to protect vulnerable people. Social workers will be working closely with numerous other professionals and agencies and this can create a tension of respecting confidentiality yet ensuring that communication is as open and transparent as possible. Partnership working and effective communication can help professionals to manage professional dilemmas but there may be a compromise needed between the external constraints and the social work ethics and values. As mentioned earlier in the chapter, a central strand within the ethical fabric of personalisation is the concept of co-production and the need to reverse the thinking about service user dependency on public funding. When reflecting on the tight eligibility controls on access to social care funding it is clear that service users, carers, relatives and local services are essential partners who can keep society functioning and supplement the full range of resources that may be needed. Support brokerage is becoming widespread as an approach which can be provided by the local authority, an independent agency or directly by a family member to offer direct support to the individual in setting up an individual budget (Phillips 2011: 339). 'Coalition for Independent Living' (CIL), is an independent nationally based, social enterprise which was set up by disabled people to provide independent user-led brokerage models. CIL was set up to bridge the gap between disabled people and social care professionals to create user-led brokerage: 'At first I was really scared about the prospect of working for myself but now I have had the training and the support and I know that my peer support network will always be there, I know I'm not alone. I really relish the idea of running my own business' (Skills for Care; Increasing Choice; mapping the journey for brokerage, 2010). This final word from a service user who has moved from a position of dependency to interdependency with peers and professionals is a positive note to end on.

This chapter has reflected widely on the ethics and values embedded within personalisation as an ideology, a set of personal experiences and a politically driven ethos of providing adult social support. The synthesis of ideas has explored many dimensions from the service user, the social worker, the carer and partnership models. There has been reflection on the traditional social work code of practice, the values embedded in practice and the ways that personalisation has both challenged and heightened the relevance of the ethics and values intrinsic to the social work role. There has been an exploration of the public understanding of personalisation and power differentials for adults who may be discriminated against by society due to disability or old age and the scope that personal approaches to supporting people has in reducing the marginalisation of vulnerable adults. This has been linked to the theory base of citizenship and the shared emphasis between citizenship and person centred support on empowering people to have more control and choice in their lives. Finally, the chapter has considered the challenges to the social work profession which are directly linked to the transformation of adult social care services and the longer term impact on the social work role. Personalisation has been a catalyst for change requiring social work practitioners to develop a different set of skills and qualities. Ethical dilemmas in practice have been included as a way to reflect on what some of these skills and qualities may be and how practitioners can work very differently with service users and carers. Practitioners can help to achieve this through use of reflection and critical analysis to develop professional resilience and partnership working and the central role of co-production in breaking down the barriers between professionals and recipients of social care support.

References

A Lifetime of Caring (2005) Older family carers and their adult sons and daughters with learning disabilities. How can services best meet their needs? www.lifetimecaring.org.uk (accessed).

Adams, R., Dominelli, L. and Payne, M. (2008) *Social Work and Power.* Basingstoke: Palgrave Macmillan.

Barnett, M. (2006) Social constructivism. In J. Bayliss and S. Smith (eds) *Globalism of World Politics.* Oxford: Oxford University Press.

BASW (2012) *The Code of Ethics for Social Work: A Statement of Principles.* www.policy@basw. co.uk (accessed).

Beresford, P. (2011) *A Warning: don't give up your day job to be an unpaid carer.* Guardian joepublic blog. www.guardian.co.uk. (accessed 24th February 2011).

Beresford, P. and Croft, S. (2001) Service user's knowledge and the social construction of social work. *Journal of Social Work*, 1(3):

Blackman, N. and Todd, S. (2005) *A Guide for Professionals Offering Palliative Care and Support.* London: Worth Publishing.

Bolton, G. (2010) *Reflective Practice; Writing and Professional Development*, 3rd edn. London: Sage.

Burton, J. (2010) Call it personalisation if you like. *Social Work Practice*, 24(3): 301–13.

Cleary, J. (2010) Social work, the personalisation agenda and transformation of services. Paper presented at the Skills for Care Conference, London, October.

Davies, M. (1999) *The Blackwell Companion to Social Work.* Oxford: Blackwell.

Department for Work and Pensions (2005) *Opportunity Age: Meeting the Challenges of Ageing in the 21st Century.* London: DWP.

DH (Department of Health) (1990) *NHS and Community Care Act.* London: HMSO.

DH (2007) *Putting People First: A Shared Vision and Commitment to the Transformation of Adult Social Care.* London: DH.

DH (2010) *Social Work Reform Board – One Year On.* Department of Health 2010 ref. 15294 www.dh.gov.uk. (accessed 14th December 2010).

Duffy, S. (2006) *Keys to Citizenship*, 2nd ed. Centre for Welfare Reform.

Duffy, S. (2010) The citizenship theory of social justice: exploring the meaning of personalisation for social workers. *Social Work Practice*, 24(3): 253–65.

Ferguson, I. (2007) Increasing user choice or privatising risk? The antinomies of personalisation. *British Journal of Social Work*, 37(3): 387–403.

Gaylard, D. (2010) in C. Gaine (2010) *Equality and Diversity in Social Work Practice.* Exeter: Learning Matters.

Glasby, J. and Littlechild, R. (2009) *Direct Payments and Personal Budgets: Putting Personalisation into Practice.* Bristol: Policy Press.

Healy, K. and Mulholland, J. (2007) *Writing Skills for Social Workers.* Social Work in Action.

Hirst, M. (2000) *Access to Healthcare for Carers: Barriers and Interventions.* York: Social Policy Research, University of York.

Jones, T. (1993) *British Ethnic Minorities: Student Edition.* Policy Studies Institute.

Jordan, B. (1990) *Social Work in an Unjust Society.* Brighton: Harvester Wheatsheaf.

Koprowska, J. (2010) *Communication and Interpersonal Skills in Social Work,* 3rd edn. Exeter: Learning Matters.

Langan, M. and Lee, P. (1989) *Radical Social Work Today.* London: Unwin Hyman.

Le Grand, J., Popper, C. and Smith, S. (2008) *The Economics of Social Problems,* 4th edn. Basingstoke: Palgrave Macmillan.

Maher, J. and Green, H. (2002) *Informal Care.* London: The Kings Fund Centre.

Mandelstam, M. (2009) *Safeguarding Vulnerable Adults and the Law.* London: Jessica Kingsley.

Manthorp, J., Jacobs, S., Rappaport, J. et al. (2008) Training for change: early days of individual budgets and the implications for social work and care management practice. *British Journal of Social Work*, 11(4): 422–38.

Oliver, M. (1990) *The Politics of Disablement.* Basingstoke: Macmillan.

Phillips, T. (2011) *Support Brokerage and Family Support*. National Brokerage Network, Eastern Region. info@nationalbrokeragenetwork.org.uk (accessed).

Rogowski, S. (2010) *Social Work; The Rise and Fall of a Profession?* Bristol: Policy Press.

Schön, D. (1983) *The Reflective Practitioner*. New York: Basic Books.

SCIE (2008/10) *Personalisation: A Rough Guide*. London: SCIE.

Sibley, D. (1997) *Geographies of Exclusion*. London and New York: Routledge.

Smale, G., Tuson, G. and Statham, D. (2000) *Social Work and Social Problems*. Basingstoke: Palgrave Macmillan.

Thompson, N. (1993) *Anti-Discriminatory Practice*. Basingstoke: Macmillan.

Titterton, M. (2005) *Risk and Risk Taking in Health and Social Welfare*. London: Jessica Kingsley.

Tyson, A. (2011) Personalisation without bureaucracy. *Community Care*, 22.

Webster, K. (2008) A yes man no more: from a service to a life. *Learning Disability Today*, July: 32–4.

2

Social and political influences

Introduction

Personalisation is not just about a new way of 'doing things' or delivering a service but it is primarily a new philosophical paradigm within the public sector. It has come about by changes that have emerged both in social work as a profession and in the way political philosophy has developed since the 1980s. The much quoted infamous remark of Baron Douglas Jay (*The Socialist Case*, 1937), 'in the case of nutrition and health, just as in the case of education, the gentleman in Whitehall really does know better what is good for people than the people know themselves' was in some way indicative of the thinking that may have existed at the time. However, both social work and political philosophy have come a long way from a view of people and especially service users as passive recipients of services to the concept of personalisation, which promotes a completely different view of service users as being the experts in their own right capable of making active choices. In politics, policy and in social work there has been a movement from paternalistic approaches to the notion of consumer-citizen (more about this later in this chapter).

Social work in the UK is intrinsically linked with legislation and government policy so changes in policy impact the way services are provided. But social work itself has changed over the years from a charity model to an empowerment model. While there have always been some tensions between how social workers see themselves and what policy makers think social workers should do, in personalisation we see, to some extent, a coming together of the agendas of social work as a profession and the agenda of government. One must add, though, that while this seeming shared agenda is at least evident in what is being professed as the way forward in delivering services to the most vulnerable in society, in practice there is much to be done to make this vision of service user empowerment a reality. These challenges will be discussed in more detail in later chapters.

Learning outcomes for this chapter

1   To understand the sociological milieu within which personalisation emerged
2   To understand the evolution of political philosophy leading to personalisation
3   To understand the legislative and policy framework for personalisation

Understanding personalisation from the social work perspective

---

CASE STUDY 2.1

Louise is a 17-year-old young person with autism and severe learning disability. Louise has been living with her parents who are very religious. The family feel that Louise is their responsibility and so have never approached Children's Services for any support. The church that the family go to provide some financial support to the family and some church members have also drawn up a rota for volunteers to care for Louise and take her out into the community.

As Louise approaches adulthood her needs have changed and it has become much more difficult to manage her behaviour, which is often very aggressive. The volunteers now do not feel safe taking her out into the community. Also the demands of her personal care have increased and her parents, who are also now ageing, are finding it difficult to cope.

A family friend has suggested contacting the transition team to start linking Louise in with adult social care. The family are reluctant to contact adult social care and would prefer to support Louise themselves and through the church volunteers.

Questions to consider

1   What do you think is the view of the family regarding Louise, her disability and the way to support her?
2   What do you think would be the perspective of the family friend about the situation?
3   What do you think might be the perspective of a social worker in this situation?

The discussion above may have highlighted various ways of approaching the situation. The family believe that Louise has been 'given' to them for a purpose and so they need to take full responsibility for her needs with some input from the church and/or other charitable organisations. The social worker might think about completing an assessment of need to identify unmet needs and may also be concerned about Louise's safety given that she has a range of different and untrained volunteers taking her out into the community. For a young person with autism this can be particularly difficult to cope with.

In an ideal world, personalisation would be a useful way forward as it in some ways brings together the way an individual would like to be supported and ensures this can happen in a safe, planned and enabling way.

The historical context of social work

In order to fully appreciate the almost revolutionary change that the promise of personalisation holds out, it is important to delve very briefly into the history of social work to understand how perspectives have changed leading to change in practice of social work.

The desire to help others has probably existed as long as the human race itself, but the right way to help in the most effective way has been constantly debated and as a result changed over history. The following timeline of the evolution of social work adapted from *Evolution of Social Welfare/Work* by Rengasamy (2009) demonstrates how perspectives of social work and therefore practice of social work have changed over time:

313 Christianity was legalized by the Roman Emperor, Constantine. The Church was authorised to use donated funds to aid the poor. Charitable attitudes and behaviours were expected of the rich.

By 590 the Church had a system for distributing aid to the poor through the office of the deacon. As there was no effective bureaucracy below city government that was capable of charitable activities, the clergy served this role in the West up through the eighteenth century.

1500s Henry VIII in England broke away from the Roman Catholic Church. The State confiscated Church wealth, leaving it without means to carry out charity expectations.

1536 The Henrician Poor Law, also known as the Act for the Punishment of Sturdy Vagabonds and Beggars, was established. The government of Henry VIII classified types of poor people and established procedures for collecting voluntary donations and disbursing funds. The law required that these procedures be carried out at the local rather than the national level. It also acknowledged that the state rather than the church or volunteers must play some role in caring for poor people.

1572 England could no longer depend on voluntary contributions to care for its poor people. A national tax, the Parish Poor Rate, was levied to cover these costs. This was accompanied by a register of people needing relief. Funds left over from poor relief were used to create jobs for people deemed fit to work.

1601 The Elizabethan Poor Law was established. Built on the experiments of the earlier Henrician Poor Law (1536) and the Parish Poor Rate (1572), this legislation became the major codification of dealing with the poor and disadvantaged for over two hundred years. Taxes that people paid in each parish paid for their own poor, established apprentice programs for poor children and developed workhouses for dependant people. The law dealt harshly and punitively with people who were poor but considered fit to work.

1600s Poor Law principles were introduced to New World by Plymouth colonists. The poor and unfortunate were divided into two groups: 'deserving' sick, disabled, widows, orphans and the elderly who had saved for themselves; and "undeserving" offenders, unmarried mothers, vagrants, unemployed and the old without savings.

1697 The workhouse system was developed in Bristol and soon spread throughout England and parts of Europe. It was designed to keep down poor taxes by denying aid to anyone who refuses to enter a workhouse. These institutions were usually managed by private entrepreneurs who contracted with the legal authorities to care for the residents in exchange for using their work.

Residents – including very young children, disabled people and older people – were often given minimal care and had to work long hours as virtual slaves.

1834 The new Poor Law was established in England to reform the Elizabethan Poor Law (1601). The underlying emphasis of the new law was on self-reliance. Public assistance is not considered a right, and government is not seen as responsible for those who were unemployed. The principles of 'less eligibility' and 'perception of need' were embedded in society's attitudes toward the poor and less able. The principle of 'less eligibility' (a recipient of aid can never receive as much as does the lowest-paid worked) was enforced.

Charity Organisation Societies (COS) formed in England with an emphasis on detailed investigations. Volunteers were recruited to befriend applicants, make individual assessments and 'correct' their problems. This was the precursor for professionalisation of social work.

1958 Working Definition of Social Work Practice, headed by Harriett Bartlett, defines person-in-environment as social work's comprehensive domain of practice; published in 1970 by Bartlett in Common Base of Social Work.

1982 Global definition of social work approved by the 44 nation members of International Federation of Social Workers (IFSW) was as follows: 'Social work is a profession whose purpose it is to bring about social changes in society in general and in its individual forms of development' (IFSW 1982).

2000 A new definition of social work was accepted by the General Meeting in Montreal in 2000 and then formally adopted by both the International Association for Schools of Social Work (IASSW) and IFSW in May 2001, as follows:

> 'The social work profession promotes social change, problem-solving in human relationships, and the empowerment and liberation of people to enhance well-being. Utilising theories of human behaviour and social systems, social work intervenes at the points where people interact with their environments. Principles of human rights and social justice are fundamental to social work.'

The definitions reveal how social work saw itself and how it evolved.

2001 The General Social Care Council was established in October 2001 under the Care Standards Act 2000 and was a Non Departmental Public Body. The GSCC is responsible for setting standards of conduct and practice for social care workers and their employers.

Among other things, the GSCC Code of Practice set out in 2004 and updated in 2010 affirms the need for social workers to protect the rights and promote the interests of service users and carers; promote the independence of service users and respect the rights of service users. (GSCC Codes of Practice 2002).

The historical perspective outlined above demonstrates how social work has evolved from a charity model espoused by religious organisations to a model that promotes independence and respects service users' rights and choices with the involvement of the state and professionalization of social work. Personalisation in its purest form is a way for social work to put into practice its vision of empowered service users who are able to choose how they receive a service and how services should be provided to make the most difference in their lives.

Understanding personalisation within the political philosophical debate

Hampton (1997) suggests that political philosophy is not any surface description of particular political societies but seeks to understand foundation of states at the deepest level. It is therefore important to understand the political underpinnings for person-alisation before going into what works or does not work in practice or the implemen-tation of personalisation. Like any new initiative personalisation is bound to face resistance or be viewed with some scepticism. But what is important is to look at the philosophical foundations and see if one agrees with those foundations or not. If one accepts the philosophical foundations for personalisation then one is more likely to embrace it and be committed to work through the practical problems that it might present. This section will therefore to look at the changing political perspectives that lead to personalisation.

Reflective exercise 2.1

List the key characteristics/values of the Conservative Party, the Labour Party and The Liberal Democrats.

The traditional understanding of the political landscape is that various political principles lie on a line between the left and the right. Traditionally the left believes in equality and promotes some form of socialism where the state has a very important role in ensuring equality. The right are those who believe in freedom and would promote free market capitalism believing that people should be free to make their own decisions and the role of the state should be minimal. In the middle are those who would advocate a mixture of equality and freedom and would therefore endorse some form of welfare-state capitalism (Kymlicka 1990). In practice however there are a range of other political views that do not fit in with any specific traditional political position.

Table 2.1 shows a table of voter turnout at general elections since 1945. It is interesting to note that after 1997 there seems to be a significant drop in voter turnout at general elections. During the general elections in 2010 the BBC interviewed potential voters about who they were likely to vote for and many said that they would not bother to vote because they did not find that there was much of a difference between the various political parties, so it did not really matter who came to power.

While there certainly might be a range of reasons for lower turnouts recently it is important to look at the changing political landscape with the emergence of New Labour which to some extent continued to blur the battle lines between the traditional arch rivals – The Conservatives and Labour.

Catherine Bochel et al.'s (2005) analysis of government under the Conservatives from 1979 to 1997 suggests that there would appear to be two phases. Until 1988 there was an emphasis on 'managerialism' where it was believed that private sector business performance tools could be transferred to the public sector to bring about more efficiency. From around 1988, a new style of governance emerged that was based on 'the new institutional economics' with concepts such as markets and consumer choice being central. The key change in this form of governance was the involvement of a wider range of organisations including the public sector, private sector and voluntary agencies in service implementation and delivery.

Table 2.1 General election turnout since 1945, by region

Year	UK	England	Wales	Scotland	N.Ireland
1945	72.8	73.4	75.7	69	67.4
1950	83.9	84.4	84.8	80.9	77.4
1951	82.6	82.7	84.4	81.2	79.9
1955	76.8	76.9	79.6	75.1	74.1
1959	78.7	78.9	82.6	78.1	65.9
1964	77.1	77	80.1	77.6	71.7
1966	75.8	75.9	79	76	66.1
1970	72	71.4	77.4	74.1	76.6
1974 Oct	72.8	72.6	76.6	74.8	67.7
1974 Feb	78.8	79	80	79	69.9
1979	76	75.9	79.4	76.8	67.7
1983	72.7	72.5	76.1	72.7	72.9
1987	75.3	75.4	78.9	75.1	67
1992	77.7	78	79.7	75.5	69.8
1997	71.4	71.4	73.5	71.3	67.1
2001	59.4	59.2	61.6	58.2	68
2005	61.4	61.3	62.6	60.8	62.9
2010	65.1	65.5	64.7	63.8	57.6

Source: House of Commons Research Papers 01/54, 05/33 and 10/36 (accessed from: www.ukpolitical.info)

The neoliberal Conservative government emphasised the role of market forces in developing communities that were in decline. There was an increased emphasis on social market as well as the private market which showed itself in a range of partnerships with local authorities and with communities. Funding was made available that local authorities could compete for like the Estates Renewal Challenge and Single Regeneration Budget, where local communities were engaged in planning the regeneration of their areas and in the implementation of these plans. The key development here was that members of the community had more of a say and were more able to participate in decisions affecting their area (Somerville 2011).

When the Labour government came to power in 1997 under the banner of New Labour, the pace of changes to partnership between public, private and voluntary sectors accelerated. New Labour continued to see 'communities as actors in the market, helping to shape that market in their own interest, through choices they make as individual and collective consumers' (Bochel 2005).

Firm Foundations (CLG 2004) is an important publication that shows how the New Labour government saw the role of citizens and community groups as being very important in shaping services that would affect them and determining the quality of their life.

In his speech to the 2002 Labour Party annual conference, the then Labour Prime Minister Tony Blair said,

Just as mass production has departed from industry, so monolithic provision of services has to depart from the public sector. People want an individual service for them. They want Government under them not over them. They want Government to empower them, not control them. And they want equality of both opportunity and responsibility. Out goes the big state. In comes the enabling state.

(www.staff.city.ac.uk/p.willetts/IRAQ/INDEX.HTM)

Adams (Bochel 2005) suggests that Labour sought to restructure personal social services based on the individual rather than need as defined by agencies. This implied organising services around the needs and expectations of service users rather than starting with a large bureaucracy providing services.

It is against this political backdrop that the development of personalisation must be viewed as an initiative that believes that individuals and communities know best what their needs are and therefore are best placed to use resources judiciously to meet those needs. This historical perspective also demonstrates why there is agreement between the Conservatives and Labour parties around personalisation and with it a commitment to fund it even in difficult economic times.

Before we move on to the legislation and policy that makes personalisation possible it is important to consider two key concepts without which a deep understanding of personalisation would be difficult: participation and customer-citizenship.

1 Participation

Reflective exercise 2.2

Define participation and list five activities that would demonstrate participation of service users in your work as a social worker.

Share your responses with a partner.

It is difficult to have a definition of participation that everyone agrees on but broadly speaking participation means being involved. Levels of participation would differ based on the context and the stake one has. For example, people would tend to participate much more in their home, that is, being involved in the various tasks that need to be done to keep the home running and also being involved in decisions for the well-being of all members of the family.

When it comes to participation in life, in society it again depends on what the stakes are. For example, a parent of a disabled young person will be more inclined to participate in forums where decisions are being made regarding services for people with disabilities but someone with no disabled person in their family is less likely to participate. In the social and political arena there is much professed emphasis on participation. Governments want themselves to be seen as opening the possibilities for people to participate more and more so that decisions and services would be more fit for purpose.

But participation can be tokenistic, a delaying tactic or a ruse to legitimise a decision through ineffective participation where involvement is used to give an appearance of agreement (Croft and Beresford 1996).

In trying to understand the real meaning of true participation, Arnstein's (1969) 'ladder of citizen partnership' is very helpful.

8   Citizenship control
7   Delegated power   } degrees of citizen power
6   Partnership

5   Placation
4   Consultation } degrees of tokenism
3   Informing

2   Therapy   } non-participation
1   Manipulation

The lowest level of participation is really non-participation because people have no real say in or influence on decisions made. Participants are expected to go along with decisions made by others and are powerless to make changes themselves. The next level suggests that people have some involvement, but other people make important decisions and inform members about new policies or what action to take. The top level suggests that people are in positions of influence, that they have a say in decision making and that their opinions are taken into account and acted upon. The political process of personalisation hopes that people would participate at the highest level because they would have direct control of resources and therefore exercise control over how their needs are met.

2 Customer-citizenship

During their time in power from 1979 to 1997, Conservative governments emphasised citizens' rights to freedom and choice. There was a commitment to promoting customer choice and there was fierce criticism of the public sector, which was seen to ignore individual needs of citizens. There was political consensus around the concept of customer-citizen with the Labour Party also emphasising the need to empower individuals as consumers against the dominance of the state in their lives (Harris and White 2009).

The Labour Party came to power in 1997, calling themselves New Labour, and embarked on a journey of modernising social services and this meant that the way forward for the public sector was to promote diversity of providers and customer choice. The document *Service First* issued by the Cabinet Office in 1998 set out expectations about standards of service, provision of information, access and choice, effective resource use and collaboration with a range of service providers.

The modernisation agenda sought to make social services more business-like and treat people who use services more like customers (Harris 2003). In this new way of looking at service users, they were no longer passive recipients but active choice makers. Customer-citizenship can therefore be seen as very important in the context of personalisation where the potential for choice and control reaches far beyond any previous model of service delivery.

Leadbeater (2004) puts the concept of customer-citizen at a different level when he says

> Public service users should have a voice directly in the service as it is delivered. That voice will be unlocked only if they also have a degree of choice over when, where, how and to what end a service is delivered. The aim of personalised public services is not to provide the self interested, self-gratification of consumerism but to build a sense of self-actualisation, self realisation and self-enhancement.

The legislative and policy framework for personalisation

So far we have looked at the development in the understanding of social work and in the political spheres that led to creating fertile ground where personalisation could be rolled out with a fair chance of success. In this section we will look at the development of legislation and policy that makes personalisation possible.

Key legislation leading up to personalisation

The National Assistance Act 1948

After the Second World War, the period from 1945 to 1948 was significant in terms of social policy since it heralded the introduction of a truly comprehensive welfare state in Britain. (Johns 2011). In 1948 the Poor Law was repealed and replaced by a national scheme for payment of social security benefits and new legislation to provide for older people and disabled people. The first piece of legislation directed to adults requiring support was the National Assistance Act 1948 which heralded the introduction of the welfare state. The Act divided the financial and non-financial welfare of those in need. Financial welfare was dealt with by the National Assistance Board and non-financial welfare of older people and disabled people was now the remit of the local authority. Social security was about provision of cash to people in need and social services were to provide in-kind assistance (Glasby and Littlechild 2002).

The National Health Service and Community Care Act 1990

As we have seen earlier in this chapter, the political philosophy prevalent in the 1980s was that of encouraging more partnership between the public sector, private sector and the voluntary sector. There was also more of an awareness of the need for more joined-up working among public sector agencies. So it was not surprising therefore, that when the NHS and Community Care Act 1990 was passed there was a greater emphasis on opening up to market forces. Now the local authority did not necessarily have to provide services itself but was able to use independent service providers. In fact one of the six key Government objectives that a care plan was to meet was to promote the development of a flourishing independent sector alongside quality public services.

In many ways, although the National Health Service and Community Care (NHS and CC) Act 1990 was charting new territory as it recognised that it was possible for service users to play a more active part in the management of their care, it did not allow for service users to have any control of resources. This was despite campaigning for direct payments by advocates of independent living already being underway before the NHS and CC Act was passed and there was also serious lobbying to have direct payments included in the Act. But unfortunately this back-fired and local authorities were actually reminded of section 29 of the 1948 Act that prohibited local authorities from making cash payments in place of arranging services (Glasby and Littlechild 2002).

The Community Care (Direct Payments) Act 1996

Although the campaign for direct payments received a setback with the NHS and CC Act 1990 making it illegal, the campaign continued to receive support from many other bodies like the Association of Directors of Social Services (ADSS). In 1992, ADSS adopted a resolution in support of direct payments which said, 'This association requests that Local Authorities be empowered, following an assessment of need, to make direct payments to disabled people in order that they can buy and organise their own services, allowing personal autonomy and control' (quoted in Taylor 1996).

In 1994, the British Council of Organisations of Disabled People (BCODP) published a piece of research by Zarb and Nadesh titled 'Cashing in on independence' which emphasized the positive aspects of direct payments for disabled people. In November 1994, the government announced its intention to legislate to allow local authorities to provide direct payments instead of themselves providing community care services.

The Community Care (Direct Payments) Act 1996 gave local authorities the power (not duty) to make direct payments. Since this was a new initiative, there were restrictions put in place to ensure that abuse was limited. Direct payments could only be made to disabled people between 18 and 65 years of age and if the local authority was satisfied that they were 'willing' to receive payments instead of services and were 'able' to manage the financial and legal implications that direct payments brought with it.

Gradually as the government became more satisfied of the effectiveness and even cost efficiency of direct payments there was more relaxation of the restrictions through new regulation on 1 February 2000 and people aged over 65 also became eligible for direct payments.

The Carers and Disabled Children Act 2000 made it possible for local authorities to provide direct payments to carers and parents of disabled children.

Key policy in the development of personalisation

The year 2000 was the start of a decade that focused on making services more responsive to the individual with several policy papers coming out that led to personalised budgets becoming a reality:

Valuing People 2001

The 2001 White Paper *Valuing People: A New Strategy for Learning Disability for the 21st century* was key in the run up to personalisation because it set out the importance of person centred planning which was seen as vitally important in the process of personalisation.

This paper set out 11 objectives aimed at improving the lives of people living with disabilities and intended to result in improvements in education, social services, health, employment, housing and support for people with learning disabilities and their families and carers. The proposals in the White Paper are based on four key principles: civil rights, independence, choice and inclusion. All of these form the basis for personalisation in the future.

Valuing People takes a lifelong approach, beginning with an integrated approach to services for disabled children and their families and then providing new opportunities for a full and purposeful adult life.

In Control 2003 (not a policy document)

As the sub-heading states this is not a policy document! However, it is important to mention In Control which was founded in 2003 by a small group of people who wanted to make life better for local families with disabled members in Wigan, Lancashire. In Control has since gone on to become an independent social enterprise with charitable status. In Control pioneered the concept of self directed support and developed individual budgets as a way for people to take charge of their support. In Control piloted the self directed support model across six areas of England, bringing real, sustainable benefits with no increase in costs.

Between 2005 and 2007, this work strongly influenced Government policy and resulted in Putting People First, a national policy which introduced personal budgets and is helping to transform adult social care for the better.

Our Health, Our Care, Our Say: A New Direction for Community Services 2006

The fact that the pioneering work of In Control and its proven success with individual budgets greatly influenced government policy is borne out in this White Paper (DH 2006) which extended the programme of direct payment and introduced a collaborative approach to the provision of individual budgets. Here it must be emphasised that individual budgets bring together funding streams besides social care funding. Service users eligible for individual budgets could take it as cash or as a service or a combination of cash and services depending on what worked best for them.

This White Paper outlined three themes:

- putting people more in control of their own health and care;
- enabling and supporting health, independence and well-being;
- rapid and convenient access to high-quality, cost-effective care.

It also seven outcomes outlined:

- improved health and emotional well-being;
- improved quality of life;
- making a positive contribution;

- choice and control;
- freedom from discrimination;
- economic well-being;
- personal dignity.

This truly was a new direction because it sought to change the way services were provided making services more tailored to the individual offering more choice, control and flexibility.

Putting People First: A Shared Vision and Commitment to the Transformation of Adult Social Care 2007

This ministerial concordat acknowledges that the community care legislation of 1990 was well intentioned but led to a system which can be over complex and often fails to respond to peoples' needs and expectations. It says that this landmark protocol seeks to set out and support the Government's commitment to independent living for all adults. It seeks to be the first public service reform programme which is co-produced, co-developed, co-evaluated and recognises that real change will only be achieved through the participation of users and carers at every stage (HM Government 2007).

This is a ministerial concordat that focuses on how to ensure that an individual eligible for services get the best quality service in the most flexible way, exercising maximum choice and control.

This will be done first of all by every locality seeking

> to have a single community based support system focussed on the health and wellbeing of the local population. Binding together local Government, primary care, community based health provision, public health, social care and the wider issues of housing, employment, benefits advice and education/training. This will not require structural changes, but organisations coming together to re-design local systems around the needs of citizens.
>
> (HM Government 2007).

This means there would be a system where organisations work around people rather than people trying to work their way around organisations.

In the reformed system, the right to self-determination will be at the centre and this will be achieved by personal budgets which will ensure people receiving public funding use available resources to choose their own support services and will increasingly shape and commission their own services.

Putting People First is underpinned by four key themes:

1 Access to universal services such as transport, leisure and education as well as information, advice and advocacy: This means that due consideration should be given when planning for these to consider the implications for disabled and older people

2 Prevention and early intervention: This involves helping people early enough or in the right way, so that they stay healthy and recover quickly from illness

3   Choice and control – people who need support can design it themselves, under-
    standing quickly how much money is available for this, and having a choice about
    how they receive support and who manages it

4   Social capital – making sure that everyone has the opportunity to be part of a
    community and experience the friendships and care that can come from families
    and friends.

(http://www.idea.gov.uk/idk/aio/14007769)

Putting People First, therefore seeks to reform the system to make it more responsive
to the needs of the people it serves by putting people at the centre. The key to true
empowerment is the willingness to put resources directly in the hands of service users
believing that service users know best how to use resources effectively to meet their
individual outcomes for an independent and fulfilled life.

Valuing People Now 2009

Valuing People: The Story So Far (Greig 2005: 3), reporting on progress, identified
the inclusion of people with complex needs as a challenge and stated that: 'What often
happens for people with complex needs is that either they are forgotten – perhaps
because they are less able to speak up for themselves – or else services respond to their
needs by putting them in separate services' (Cooper and Ward 2011: 39).

As part of the *Valuing People Now* consultation the Department of Health received
clear messages from families and others that many people with complex needs were
not benefiting from *Valuing People*.

Valuing People Now (DH 2009) sought to reflect these concerns with a new three-
year strategy for people with learning disabilities. This strategy addresses what people
said about the support people with learning disabilities and their families need and
reflects the changing priorities across government which impact directly on people with
learning disabilities; namely, including everyone, personalisation and, health care for all.

Other relevant legislation

Mental Capacity Act 2005

Since people with learning disabilities are also entitled to a personal budget an obvious
concern raised would be around the person's capacity to agree to have a personal
budget. This is where it would be important to have recourse to the Mental Capacity
Act 2005 and adhere to principles set out in the Act which are as follows:

- A person must be assumed to have capacity unless it is established that he lacks
  capacity.

- A person is not to be treated as unable to make a decision unless all practicable
  steps to help him to do so have been taken without success.

- A person is not to be treated as unable to make a decision merely because he
  makes an unwise decision.

- An act done or decision made, under this Act for or on behalf of a person who
  lacks capacity must be done, or made, in his best interests.

- Before the act is done, or the decision is made, regard must be had to whether the purpose for which it is needed can be as effectively achieved in a way that is less restrictive of the person's rights and freedom of action.

(Mental Capacity Act 2005)

Human Rights Act 1998

Personalisation can be seen as a way of promoting and upholding the human rights of the most vulnerable in society. This is particularly true of the right enshrined in article 8: the right to respect for private and family life, home and correspondence (Human Rights Act 1998). Personalisation reduces interference of the state in people's private life while also providing the means to have as independent and fulfilled a life as possible.

Chapter summary

The understanding of social work and therefore the practice of social work has evolved through history. The beginnings of social work were in well-intentioned charitable endeavours of the well-off in society towards the less fortunate, and this was often accompanied by the belief that the ones providing the resources were most know-ledgeable about how best those resources were used for the poor. But over time these paternalistic approaches gave way to models of empowerment where resources and therefore power were transferred to the service user.

Similarly in politics there has been a movement from Big Government to Big Society where governments increasingly seek to put power in the hands of people. Where in the 1970s the government held the responsibility of providing services with little flexibility there was gradually a movement towards personalising services. This was achieved to gradually involving the private sector and voluntary agencies in service provision to finally putting resources in the hands of service user, who could decide what to buy, when and how in order to meet their outcomes for an independent and fulfilled life.

Finally, for the transformation in social and political thinking to take root, it has to be backed by legislation and policy. Since 1990, successive pieces of legislation and policy have mirrored the social and political pulse by ensuring that people who use services have more choice and control. Legislation has been fought for by incessant lobbying, research evidence and not least by the voice of the customer-citizen of this generation.

References

Arnstein, S. (1969) A ladder of citizen participation. *Journal of the American Institute of Planners*, 35(4) July.

Bochel, H., Bochel, C., Page, R. and Sykes, R. (2005) *Social Policy: Issues and Developments*. Harlow: Pearson Prentice Hall.

CLG (2004) Firm Foundations: The Government's Framework for Community Capacity Building, Together We Can Conference, December.

Cooper, V. and Ward, C. (2011) Valuing people now and people with complex needs. *Tizard Learning Disability Review*, 16(2): 39.

Croft, S. and Beresford, P. (1996) The politics of participation, in D. Taylor (ed.) *Critical Social Policy: A Reader.* London: Sage.

DH (1990) *The NHS and Community Care Act.* London: HMSO.

DH (1996) *Community Care (Direct Payments) Act.* London: Department of Health.

DH (2001) *Valuing People: A New Strategy for Learning for the 21st Century.* London: Department of Health.

DH (2006) *Our Health, Our Care, Our Say: A New Direction for Community Service.* London: Department of Health.

DH (2005) *Mental Capacity Act*

DH (2009) *Valuing People Now: a new three-year strategy for people with learning disabilities.* London: Department of Health.

Greig, R. (2005) *Valuing People: The Story So Far*, Report. London: Department of Health.

Glasby, J. and Littlechild, R. (2002) *Social Work and Direct Payments.* Bristol: The Policy Press.

GSCC (2002) *Code of Practice for Social Worker.* London: General Social Care Council.

IDEA (date not available) Transforming Adult Social Care Delivery Support Architecture. http:dRwww.idea.gov.uk/idk/aio/14007769 (accessed on 20 August 2011).

IFSW (1982) *Definition of Social Work.* Brighton: IFSW.

Hampton, J. (1997) *Political Philosophy.* Oxford: Westview Press.

Harris, J. and White, V. (2009) *Modernising Social Work.* Bristol: The Policy Press.

Harris, J. (2003) *The Social Work Business.* London: Routledge.

HM Government (2007) *Putting People First: A shared vision and commitment to the transformation of adult social care.* London. Home Office

Jay, D. (1937) *The Socialist Case.* London: Faber and Faber.

Johns, R. (2011) *Social Work, Social Policy and Older People.* Exeter: Learning Matters.

Kymlicka, W. (1990) *Contemporary Political Philosophy*, Oxford: Oxford University Press.

Leadbeater, C. (2004) *Personalisation through Participation: A New Script for Public Services.* London: Demos.

Rengasamy, S. (2009) *Evolution of Social Welfare/Work.* Madurai: Madurai Institute of Social Sciences.

Somerville, P. (2011) *Understanding Community.* Bristol: The Policy Press.

Taylor, R. (1996) Independent Living and Direct Payments. Speech delivered to the ADSS Spring Conference, Cambridge, April.

Willets, P. (2002) Selected documents and speeches on the crisis over Iraq. www.staff.city.ac.uk/p.willets/IRAQ/INDEX.HTM (accessed 18 August 2011).

www.Ukpolitical.info

Zarb, G. and Nadash, P. (1994) *Cashing in on Independence.* The British Council of Organisations of Disabled People (BCODP).

3

Opportunities and challenges in personalisation

Introduction

Julie Jones, Chief Executive, SCIE states, 'Personalisation means thinking about public services and social care in an entirely different way – starting with the person rather than the service. It will require the transformation of adult social care.' This constitutes a huge change in the way provision of care to vulnerable adults in society is conceived and provided. Change of this magnitude is bound to be received differently by different people. Some would embrace change as an opportunity to transform social care for the better while some would have reservations about hopping unreservedly onto the personalisation band wagon. Politically, personalisation was one initiative that received unanimous support from all major political parties. The reasons for the support, though, were varied as it appealed to different people and different groups across the political spectrum. Some people are supportive of these ways of working because they see them as part of a campaign for greater civil rights, choice and control for disabled people; others see them as an essentially market-based mechanism for rolling back the boundaries of the welfare state and as a form of 'privatisation by the backdoor' (Glasby and Littlechild 2009). This chapter will look at the opportunities as seen by those optimistic about personalisation as well as the challenges as seen by those more cautious about giving personalisation their full embrace.

Personalisation presents opportunities and challenges in various areas – in the way it is conceived and perceived (the philosophical arguments for and against personalisation) and in its implementation (for social workers and other professionals, commissioners, brokers and not least for service users and carers). Personalisation is purported to be the radical reform of public services necessary to achieve a personal-ised support system that puts people first and recognises their ability to establish their own needs and how these can best be met (HM Government 2007; DH 2005, 2008). While personalisation holds the promise of more choice and control by espousing the philosophy that the service users are experts by experience and therefore know best how to use resources to meet outcomes, it is not without its share of problems that must be overcome in order to meet its goals of fully empowered service users living the life they want in the way they want.

Learning objectives for the chapter

1   To compare and contrast traditional social work models with personalisation

2   To consider the opportunities and challenges presented in terms of shedding old ways and developing new ways of care provision and the skills required for this

3   To explore the experiences of workers in the front line of personalisation, i.e. social workers, support brokers, etc. and identify what works and does not work in the implementation of personalisation

4   To examine the systems in place for rolling out personalisation and evaluate their effectiveness in making personalisation work. We will also examine the changes to the roles of commissioners

Opportunities and challenges of a new model of social work intervention

Reflective exercise 3.1

What is social work? Make a list of tasks you think a social worker would be most likely to undertake during a typical working day.

The answer to the question 'What is social work?' is likely to elicit a most diverse range of answers. The diversity of responses would be even more pronounced if the group being asked the questions was made up of individuals from different countries. The tasks undertaken by social workers would differ depending on the answer to the first question.

For social workers in the UK, the tasks you have identified might include work around safeguarding vulnerable children and adults, assessment of need, setting up packages of care to support children or adults in need and monitoring and reviewing those assessed needs. You might also have spoken of the need for meticulous record keeping and report writing, both of which take up vast amount of social work time.

So what then is social work? The following two definitions of social work might serve to highlight the differences in understanding what social work really is.

Definition 1: The social work profession promotes social change, problem solving in human relationships and the empowerment and liberation of people to enhance well-being. Utilising theories of human behaviour and social systems, social work intervenes at the points where people interact with their environments. Principles of human rights and social justice are fundamental to social work.

(International Association of Schools of Social Work and International Federation of Social Workers, 2001 in Horner, 2003)

Definition 2: Social work is a very practical job. It is about protecting people and changing their lives, not about being able to give a fluent and theoretical explanation of why they got into difficulties in the first place. New degree courses must ensure that theory and research directly informs and supports practice.

The requirements for Social Work Training set out the minimum standards for entry to social work degree courses and for the teaching and assessment that social work students must receive. The new degree will require social workers to demonstrate their practical application of skills and knowledge and their ability to solve problems and provide hope for people relying on social services for support.

(Jacqui Smith, Department of Health 2002 in Horner, 2003)

Reflective exercise 3.2

Is social work then a practical job where the social worker is responsible for setting up things for service users so that they are protected, or is it a profession that promotes social change and independence by empowering people?

The personalisation agenda brings this debate to the forefront because in some ways it forces us to rethink how social work is practised today by suggesting new systems and ways of working. A major challenge to contend with through the arrival of personalisation is the contrast between the Care Management Model and the personal, Self Directed Support Model.

Before moving on to discuss these models in detail it would be useful to clarify some of the terms being used:

Direct payments Introduced formally under 1996 legislation, the individual receives the cash equivalent of a directly provided service. This is available for social care only, and can be used to contract with a private/voluntary sector agency or to become an employer by hiring your own staff – it cannot be used to purchase public sector services.

Independent Living A key aim of the disabled people's movement has been to achieve independent living (a situation in which disabled people have as much choice and control over their lives as everyone else). This does not mean doing everything yourself – in practice, no one is truly independent, and we are all interdependent on others to meet our needs as human beings.

Indirect payments Prior to the 1996 Direct Payments Act, many local authorities overcame uncertainties in the legal context by making indirect or third party payments.

Individual/personal budget This is a new way of working pioneered by In Control. In its simplest form, it involves being clear with the person from the outset how much money is available to meet their needs, then allowing them maximum choice over how the money is spent/how much control they want over the money. Initially, the individual budgets developed by In Control were for social care funds only. Subsequently, Department of Health pilots began to explore scope for integrating a series of additional funding sources. But here as well the service user can choose to receive the money and buy equipment and services budgets. At the outset it is important to clarify the difference between individual budgets and personal budgets:

In summary, Personal Budgets refer to an upfront, transparent allocation of social care funding with service users exercising control over deciding how this is used.

There is also much greater flexibility in how it can be used. This money could be managed by councils or another organisation on behalf of individuals should they choose, or paid as a direct payment, or a mixture of both.

Individual Budget is like Personal Budget but is made up of a combination of a number of funding streams to give a more joined-up package of support. The funding streams involved in the pilot were Access to Work, Disabled Facilities Grant, the Independent Living fund, Integrated Community Equipment fund and Supporting People fund as well as social care money.

Self-directed support This is the more general term used by In Control to refer to a new system of adult social care, based around In Control's seven steps (explained later in this chapter) (Glasby and Littlechild 2009).

As a starting point to exploring the changes personalisation has brought to social work it is imperative that we reflect on the differences between the care management and the self directed model of support. Personalisation is perhaps the most significant change to the delivery of services by social workers since the NHS and community care legislation in 1990. The community care legislation at the time was seen as ground breaking in that it looked at trying to meet needs of people in need in the community rather than resorting to institutionalisation as the first recourse. The NHS and CC Act promoted the care management model of social work intervention: 'A key aspect of care management was that the process of assessment should be based on the expressed needs and preferences of the service users' (Parker: 2010).

The Care Management Model proposed a clearly laid out process that social work intervention would need to follow with service users. This was follows:

- assessment of need
- care planning
- implementation of the care plan
- monitoring the care plan
- periodic review of the care plan

Personalisation using the Self Directed Support Model, on the other hand, seeks to shift the balance of power to the service user by truly empowering the service user. In contrast to the traditional model the self directed approach has the following stages:

- self-assessment
- resource allocation system (RAS)
- support planning
- implementation of the support plan
- review

In Control further spelt this out to identify what it considers the seven key steps to self directed support:

- **Step 1** Using In Control's resource allocation system (RAS), everyone is told their financial allocation – their personal budget – and they decide what level of control they wish to take over their budget.

- **Step 2** People plan how they will use their personal budget to get the help that is best for them; if they need help to plan, then advocates, brokers or others can support them.

- **Step 3** The local authority helps people to create good support plans, checks they are safe and makes sure that people have any necessary representation. This is a particularly important part of the safeguarding process, as local authorities retain a duty of care and therefore have a key role to play in signing off support plans.

- **Step 4** People control their personal budget to the extent they want (there are currently six distinct degrees of control: ranging from direct payments at one extreme to local authority control at the other).

- **Step 5** People can use their personal budget flexibly (including for statutory services). Indeed, the only real restriction imposed is that the budget cannot be used on something illegal (as long as people are meeting their eligible needs).

- **Step 6** People can use their personal budget to achieve the outcomes that are important to them in their context of their whole life and their role and contribution within the wider community.

- **Step 7** The authority continues to check people are okay, shares what is being learned and can change things if people are not achieving the outcomes they need to achieve.

Reflective exercise 3.3

Take a look at the two models presented above, namely the Care Management Model and the Self Directed Support Model and think about these in the light of the two definitions of social work presented earlier. Does each of these models fit into any one of these definitions? Justify your answer.

The NHS and CC Act 1990 did present a new way of doing social work and it was a significant change from the past in that there was more of an emphasis on service users' needs. But looking at it from the perspective of the first definition of social work above it was not far reaching enough in terms of empowering service users. Care management, by and large, could still be seen to fit into the second definition of social work where social work is a practical job and the social worker is the protagonist of the piece doing the assessment and the setting up of the care plan and overseeing its implementation. The social worker is the expert who assesses need and devises a care package to help meet those needs. The service user is a passive recipient of services and does not know how much money is being spent.

In the self directed model, on the other hand, the empowerment aspect is more pronounced as the starting point is the service user who will complete a self assessment of their needs. This will be completed with support from a social worker who will have initially completed an assessment following referral to identify whether the person is eligible for social care support. The social worker will then apply for funding for the service user to meet the defined support needs through the Resource Allocation Scheme.

Power is where the money lies, so giving service users the power over their own budget is the ultimate rung in the ladder of empowerment. So here was an opportunity to engage in radical social work practice where root and branch transformation was possible. But this was not without its challenge of resistance both from social workers and service users who viewed the change with some scepticism.

However, a source of tension, within the self directed process has been identified by many social workers as the 'cut off' point following the assessment and allocation of funding for the service user. The stages of support, plan, design and implementation are now likely to be picked up either directly by the service user with support from their family or by a support broker. This will be discussed in more detail later in this chapter.

CASE STUDY 3.1

Jennifer is a young woman who had a good job in the financial sector in the City of London. On a weekend, Jennifer met with a serious car accident driving down to Dover for the weekend. The accident left Jennifer paralysed from the waist down. Jennifer is now a wheelchair user and needs support for her day to day personal hygiene tasks and to be able to go out into the community.

Jennifer underwent an assessment of need by a social worker in accordance with the NHS and CC Act 1990. Jennifer also needed to have an occupational therapy (OT) assessment to assess her mobility needs. Following assessment, Jennifer was offered a care package that included a carer going in at 7 am and 6 pm every day to support her with her personal care needs. Jennifer was offered access to a day centre three days a week and a care worker for six hours over the weekend to support her to go out into the community.

When the local authority began to roll out personalisation, Jennifer's social worker thought that Jennifer might be a good candidate for the pilot group for personal budget. Jennifer had mixed feeling about the idea of having a personal budget but finally agreed to put herself forward. Jennifer went through the process of assessing her own needs. The areas of need that Jennifer was required to assess were as follows:

- practical aspects of daily living;
- managing finances;
- meeting personal care needs;
- developing and maintaining positive relationships;

- getting out and about;
- work, learning and volunteering;
- staying safe from harm;
- complex needs and risks;
- eating and drinking;
- home environment;
- making important decisions about life;
- support from family carers and social support.

Having thus identified her need and having gone through the process of the self directed model above, Jennifer received a sum of money to spend on meeting her needs. The social worker proposed a number of ways in which Jennifer could go about managing her personal budget, including Jennifer doing it herself or with help from family and friends, being supported by the social worker or having a support broker to manage the budget.

Reflective exercise 3.4

- Identify the similarities and dissimilarities of the care management model and self directed support model from the perspective of the social worker.
- Identify the advantages and disadvantages of each model.

In terms of similarities, both models have an assessment as the starting point and there is planning involved. But the difference is that in the Care Management Model, the social worker is the key player in making things happen for the service user. The Self Directed Support Model, on the other hand, is more service user led and the service user is at the core of the assessment and planning process. The entire process is person centred from assessment to planning.

In social care an assessment of need is of paramount importance in determining the level of support a person is eligible for and subsequently can actually receive. In the 1980s social work assessment was largely resource led and service users assessed as needing a particular kind of service were fitted into existing services.

The reforms of the 1990s sought to make assessments more needs-led in that assessments were to identify need. But, unfortunately, again services provided were determined largely by availability of funding rather than individual need (Barnes and Mercer 2006).

In the self directed model, in a personalised system, with its focus on 'putting people first', an assessment is now no longer resource led or needs led but is person led (Leece and Leece 2011). So need is now no longer defined by the professional but by service users themselves. The self assessment process is probably the only way to ensure person-led assessment.

Self assessment, however, does present some legal challenges within the current legislative framework, i.e. the NHS and Community Care Act, as it is the duty of the local authority to assess need and eligibility for care. So until there is change in legislation the way forward is supported self-assessment where the service user takes the lead in the assessment process but the local authorities retain control of eligibility and support planning decisions.

This is again a challenge as there would be the lurking suspicion among service users of the risk of manipulation of the self directed model especially in the Resource Allocation System where it could be 'tinkered with' to make the whole exercise a money-saving opportunity.

In summary, as the document from SCIE (Carr 2010) affirms, the traditional service-led approach has often meant that people have not received the right help at the right time and have been unable to shape the kind of support they need. Personalisation is about giving people much more choice and control over their lives and goes well beyond simply giving personal budgets to people eligible for council funding. Personalisation means addressing the needs and aspirations of whole communities to ensure everyone has access to the right information, advice and advocacy to make good decisions about the support they need. There are nonetheless challenges to be overcome and as with any system, process or model the result is only as good as the commitment of individuals working within the system.

Opportunities and challenges of the changes in the role of the social worker

The source of challenges to personalisation does not only stem from a significant change in the model of social work intervention; there are practical and experiential challenges as well.

CASE STUDY 3.2

Gerry is a social worker in a local authority team who has been working with older people for over 15 years. Gerry has very good assessment skills and is able write up very detailed assessments of service users on his list of allocations. When personalisation first began to be talked about, Gerry became very anxious. He wondered how self assessment would be possible; he was sceptical about resource allocation and resulting issues around equity. Gerry was worried about people who could 'play' the system and use the self assessment system to exaggerate their level of need. Gerry was also worried about how money allocated would be used if there was no control over funds once they were disbursed.

In supervision with his line manager Gerry mentioned that he had spoken with some service users about personalisation and many older people on his case load said that they liked the current system and did not want it to change. Older people also expressed concern about the responsibility of managing money.

Gerry was also concerned about his own role as a social worker becoming defunct with the care management role becoming obsolete in the new system. Gerry was worried about becoming de-skilled and even possibly losing his job if the role of care management ceased to exist. He also felt that the personalisation agenda was really a way of cutting costs.

Questions to consider

1 Do you share Gerry's concerns about personalisation? If yes, why?
2 Are there concerns raised by Gerry that you do not agree with? What would you say to Gerry to allay his fears?

Linked research

Iain Ferguson (2007) seems to echo Gerry's fears when he argues that the popularity of the personalisation model is primarily due to its congruence with key themes of New Labour thought, including individualisation and the transfer of risk and responsibility from the state to the individual. Ferguson is of the opinion that social workers should not accept the philosophy of personalisation uncritically given its acceptance of the marketisation of social work and social care and its potential for promoting, rather than challenging, the deprofessionalisation of social work

When personalisation was first being discussed, some social workers were excited by the prospect of a new way of responding to needs of service users which held the promise of being individually tailored to meet those needs. But, understandably, the vast majority were very sceptical and sometimes even hostile to the initiative. This was largely because the role of the social worker was uncertain in the new system of personalisation. Due to the emphasis being shifted to self assessment it was envisaged that the role of assessing need would no longer be part of the social worker's remit.

Vicky White (Harris and White 2009) suggests that social workers have turned into 'unreflective people processors' by waves of a managerialism since the 1980s which has become even more pronounced with New Labour's modernisation agenda. Social workers therefore are primarily seen as a state-mediated profession with the space for radical social work being squeezed out almost completely. In recent years, therefore, social work appears to have got into a groove where professional social workers are no more able to engage in social work tasks that involved social workers being 'autonomous reflective practitioners' (Dominelli and Hoogvelt 1996). This is because the state sets the agenda within which social workers are expected to work.

In this light one can now understand Gerry's concerns because personalisation is a shift in how social work is perceived. The challenge is that there still remain aspects of the state control yet it unfolds opportunities for radical social work and for reclaiming the identity of social workers as autonomous reflective practitioners. With the advent of personalisation, although social work's subordination to statutory duties remains due to the legal underpinnings for personalisation, there is also the opportunity to drastically change the way services are provided by keeping the service user in the centre of the process.

The reduction in the social work role is slightly at odds with the social work professional capabilities framework: 'Social workers engage with individuals, families, groups and communities, working alongside people to assess and intervene.' The proposed professional capabilities framework published by the Social Work Reform Board includes intervention skills as one of its core strands. The reduction of the relationship-building element of social work may affect the emotional dimension of the work and the scope to develop empathy with users and carers. Should this be a concern or is it a change in role that the profession needs to accept and move on from?

One of Gerry's concerns is that the role social workers will occupy in this new personalised system is uncertain. It has been suggested that they will spend less time on assessment and gate-keeping and will instead be involved with support brokerage and advocacy (HM Government 2007; DH 2008).

While some local authorities see support brokerage as a function that should be undertaken by social workers who are ultimately accountable to statutory agencies there are others that believe that brokers should be accountable exclusively to individuals. This debate is further spelt out by several authors such as Beresford (2007) and Scourfield (2008).

A report by the Putting People First Consortium (Putting People First consortium 2010), the local government coalition responsible for supporting personalisation's delivery, found that personalisation has initiated significant workforce change within councils. Most authorities had undertaken 'a major workforce restructuring' that included a review of social workers' roles.

There has been an increasing role for non-social work staff because as service users take on more of a role in assessing themselves there may be less need for a professional input. There is, however, no consensus on the role of social workers in assessment. So while some councils may have delegated supported self assessment to non-social work staff, there are others that believe it is still the remit of social workers.

In the face of this uncertainty, Jo Cleary, College of Social Work interim board member and Lambeth Council's executive director of adults' and community services identifies key roles of social workers in the personalisation scenario as being more involved in safeguarding and prevention of abuse and harm and being involved in preventive work. In reflecting on the role of the social worker post personalisation, Cleary suggests 'It's something we need to look at. I don't want people to feel devalued. [But] there's a different world that we are trying to create [through personalisation] and it's not a form-filling world. It's about a different contract with the citizen.' Social work is more about direct work with people in society who are hurting and are vulnerable.

Again turning to experiences of social workers, a huge challenge is the inability to give up control which clearly presents quite a dramatic change for everyone starting with councillors, to managers, social workers and service users. For some councillors, managers and social workers there would be the challenge of relinquishing some control over the budget. In his article in *Community Care*, Jeremy Dunning's (2011) analysis is that this has sometimes resulted in an increase in bureaucracy as was revealed by a survey conducted by *Community Care* on behalf of Unison in 2011. The survey revealed that three-quarters of practitioners say there is now more bureaucracy in their roles as a result of personalisation. This was a rise of 66 per cent from the figures in the previous year's survey.

He reports one respondent as saying, 'There is a massive increase in paperwork with almost sole responsibility for social workers to complete the process. In my opinion the promotion of personalisation has been governed by managers who want to have financial control and is a contradiction of the choice principle.' Dunning again reports that Craig Dearden-Phillips, managing director of Stepping Out, an organisation dedicated to helping professionals leave the public sector to set up social enterprises, said, 'Councils have completely subverted what personal budgets are supposed to be about by their obsession with control and bizarre need to spend 50p in order to deliver a pound's worth of services'. Jeff Jerome, national director for social care transformation, admitted the level of bureaucracy is one of his 'biggest worries' in the implementation of personalisation (Dunning 2011).

The opportunity and challenge of inter-professional working

A challenge for the future of personalisation is to bring together health and social care funding through personalisation. There is a significant overlap between people who use social care and those who use the NHS and with this comes the potential for tensions but also the opportunity for more collaborative working. A significant proportion of the NHS budget is spent on people who have long-term conditions and this often includes people who already receive direct payments for their social care (Waters and Duffy 2007). But while there are indeed considerable overlaps, the policy and practice issues are actually very complex. Service users generally do not distinguish between health and social care needs (Glasby and Duffy 2007). Cornes (2011) suggests that the problem is the lack of links between policy documents that makes working together difficult.

In a session with social work students at the Bucks New University, Brian O'Shea (a service user consultant), put it very plainly when he said service users do not know and frankly do not care where the money comes from but are only interested in the resource being provided in a timely and relevant manner. So from the service user perspective an ideal situation would be health and social care professionals sorting out who pays for what and then letting the service user know what their budget entitlement is so they can get on with arranging their care, exercising choice and control (O'Shea 2011).

Experiences from the frontline

Reflective exercise 3.5

While personalisation brings with it the promise of a radically new way of providing care it may present some challenges on the frontline. Take a few minutes to identify some of the possible challenges in the implementation of personalisation.

Speaking with social workers and brokers involved in the implementation of personalisation I have been able to identify some of the challenges and opportunities experienced firsthand on the ground.

Challenges

1 Being risk averse

Institutions (in this case local authorities and health authorities) are generally cautious about 'allowing' service users to take risks. So while personalisation does not have a list of things that service users can or cannot use their budget for, in practice there are restrictions brought on by the statutory authorities funding care. Often attempts are made to justify these restrictions based on responsibility of safeguarding service users and also accountability for ensuring public funds are spent judiciously.

But more and more the idea of positive risk taking is seeping into support planning within personalisation where measured and appropriately managed risk is seen as part of life that allows growth.

2 Thinking among key players not changed

For some key players in the personalisation agenda (whether it be councillors, managers, social workers or commissioners) it is taking some time to make the shift from care provision to personalisation. This may not only be out of a reluctance to shift power and control to service users but may be due to the reluctance to accept that the 'professional' may not always know best and the service user is in fact an 'expert by experience', able to assess and judge what provision would enable them to live a more fulfilled life. Unfortunately, good policy is often thwarted by 'well-meaning' professionals who may consciously or unconsciously sabotage implementation.

One example of this is the Resource Allocation System (RAS) which actually decides how much money a service user can get. Some social workers and brokers feel that the bureaucracy within which the RAS is tied up creates difficulties because the RAS often has to go to panel where the budget can sometimes be cut. This may also be pronounced with the announcement of severe resource constraints within which local authorities have to work in the current economic scenario.

3 Time constraints

Person-centred planning affords a huge opportunity within personalisation but implementing person-centred planning and person-centred approaches does take time especially when working with service users with learning disabilities because it means spending more time with service users to understand need and help them to the extent possible to articulate those needs. This can be a challenge with pressures of workload and the temptation might be to dilute the person centred planning process. So putting the person in personalisation can often be a challenge.

The process itself can take longer as supported self assessment may not be a one sitting 90-minute care-management style assessment session but may need more time. Also until personalisation is firmly embedded the resource allocation system will take time and so will support planning.

4 Difficulty in implementation for some service users

If a service user has fluctuating needs or a condition that can deteriorate rather rapidly, personalisation can present some difficulties. For example, for a service user who experiences some episodes of mental illness at random points in a year it may be difficult to plan support. First, the self assessment will be difficult because a number of areas of need will be difficult to determine because it depends on whether the person has an episode of mental illness or not. Second, resource allocation will be complicated because one does not know in advance if and when an episode will occur.

There could also be difficulties where a service user's condition is prone to deteriorate very rapidly with little warning. In this case the allocated resource and consequently the support plan might fall short of what is actually required.

5 Supply of services

In the care management model, local authorities are monopoly purchasers. In a self directed model scenario, individual purchasers will have a very different relationship with suppliers of services. Until the market develops, service users may not have the choice personalisation proposes to offer. So service users may sometimes be in a situation where they have their budget but nothing to buy! Also, service users requiring specialist services may not have any choice if their specialist needs can only be met by one provider/professional.

Some also argue that allowing social care to face the full impact of market forces may not always be a good thing for service users. Choosing between competing providers could become confusing. But a competitive service provider market could, on the other hand, drive down costs and service users may be able to get more for their budget.

6 Lack of information on resources

In the current system there are commissioners and whole teams who have knowledge of what is available in terms of services and service providers. It can be a nightmare for service users and carers to try and navigate through the multitude of providers. Information regarding who provides what is also often not very readily available.

7 The choice not to choose

While the government would like everyone requiring social care to have a personal budget, the reality is that some may not want it because of the legal obligations that employing people brings with it including PAYE and the need to comply with the Manual Handling regulations.

Social workers and support brokers have said that many older people would prefer to receive care in the traditional way. This is because the idea of having to arrange their own care, employ personal assistants and search the market for services and providers is all too daunting. So surely, part of personalisation should be the ability to choose not to choose.

Also, the opportunity for 'exit' should be a crucial element of choice. So if a service user has opted for a personal budget, but for whatever reason wants to revert back to receiving care directly from the local authority, that element of choice should also be available.

Opportunities

In general the most positive aspects of personalisation are the choice and control it provides service users and the possibility of true empowerment through promoting the concept of customer-citizenship. Personalisation also offers the social work profession the opportunity to reclaim social work and free itself from its role of form filling bureaucrat to meaningful involvement with service users. Social workers and brokers have identified the following opportunities afforded by personalisation.

1 A new relationship between social workers/brokers and service users
Within the context of personalisation, a new relationship is possible between social workers and service users which can be summed up as a collaborative relationship. (There is more about this in the final chapter in discussions around co-production.)

2 Promotes person centred planning and person centred approaches
Personalisation is necessarily person centred so person centred planning and person centred approaches are key to its success. Notwithstanding the challenge outlined above around person centred planning being more time consuming, a majority of social workers are convinced it is the right way forward. It helps build more trusting relationships and is a way to help social workers do what they are trained to do, i.e. help people to help themselves.

3 Assessment is more practical rather than clinical
The self assessment model of personalisation looks at more practical areas of need and the assessment is simple and not overly clinical. Again here the underlying belief is that the service user is best placed to identify their needs. Although there have been concerns around manipulation and equity, by and large these have been unfounded when personalisation actually rolled out.

4 Creative practice
Personalisation offers the possibility of more creative social work practice. As mentioned in some of the challenges above, the provider market has not caught up with the speed at which personalisation has been rolled out. This offers the possibility for creativity on the part of the service user, carer and social worker to think creatively around how the personal budget can be used to achieve outcomes without having recourse to the traditional ways of service provision, such as a carer going in at fixed hours every day or attending a day centre where activities are not stimulating enough for a particular service user.

Creative support plans can go a long way in making judicious use of limited resources to meet outcomes identified by the service users in the most meaningful way.

5 Social enterprise
Social enterprises are commercially run, profit making organizations that are driven by social aims. Their profits are reinvested into social, community or environmental objectives (Business Link 2011). They are not answerable to shareholders and so the service social enterprise provides can offer more to individuals than the one-size-fits-all approach that many service users have been used to until now. Social enterprise can give something tailored and more personal that will suit the needs of the individual. Therefore, personalisation opens up opportunities for social enterprises allowing service users with a personal budget to pick and choose who should provide their services.

Chapter summary

From the above discussion we can conclude that personalisation, although an ideal to be aspired towards, is not without its challenges. But it all depends on how committed one is to attain that ideal. Leadbeater (2004) suggests that personalisation is 'a very potent but highly contested idea'. He conceptualises personalisation as existing on a continuum, where there is a 'shallow' version at one end and 'deep personalisation' at the other. According to Leadbeater, the concern around personalisation is that

> It might only mean providing better access and some limited say for users over how existing services are provided in largely traditional ways. This 'shallow' personalisation offers modest modification of mass-produced, standardised services to partially adapt them to user needs. Personalisation could just mean more 24/7 call centres, booked appointments and timely access to standardised services.
>
> 'Deep' personalisation on the other hand would give users a far greater role and also far greater responsibilities for designing solutions. It could mean promoting greater capacity for self-management and self organisation. Personalisation could be a sustaining innovation designed to make existing systems more personalised or it could be a disruptive innovation designed to put the users in the driving seat as designers and paymasters of services. It could be a programme to apply a lick of new paint to fading public services or it could be the harbinger of entirely new organisational logic.
>
> (Leadbeater 2004: 20)

In conclusion, I would like to draw on the analysis of Brian O'Shea, a service user who himself has embraced personalisation, where the challenges and opportunities of personalisation are nicely summed up as a dynamic concept in movement:

- Service users move from being clients to being citizens exercising choice and control.
- Systems and organisations move from being responsible for welfare to promoting well-being.
- Professionals see themselves no longer as experts but see their role as enabling service users to attain outcomes they want for themselves.
- The personalisation agenda does not only seek to bring about transactional change but transformational change.
- The personalisation agenda in its truest form symbolises 'freedom from' bureaucracy and professionalisation of care and moves to 'freedom to' explore, choose and achieve.
- In personalisation, social care is no longer a safety net to ensure that service users are safe and risk free but is a springboard to launch into ever new forays of challenges to live life and not merely exist.

(adapted from O'Shea 2011)

References

Barnes, C. and Mercer, G. (2006) *Independent Futures: Creating User-led Disability Services in a Disabling Society*. Bristol: Policy Press.

Beresford, P. (2007) State of independence: individual budgets, where social care users control the cash allocated to them, are being lauded: but are they just another attempt to cut costs?, *Guardian*, 23 May.

Business Link (2011) *What is Social Enterprise?* http://www.bllondon.com/SocialEnterprise/Whataresocialenterprises/SESocialEnterprises.aspx (accessed 22 October 2011).

Carr, S. (2010) *Personalisation: A Rough Guide*. London: SCIE.

Cornes, M. (2011) The challenge of managing change: what can we do differently to ensure personalisation? *Journal of Integrated Care*, 19(2): 22–9.

DH (Department of Health) (2005) *Independence, Well-Being and Choice: Our Vision for the Future of Social Care for Adults in England*, Social Care Green Paper. London: Department of Health.

DH Department of Health (2008) *Local Authority Circular LAC (DH) (2008) 1: Transforming Social Care*. London: Department of Health.

Dominelli, L. and Hoogvelt, A. (1996) Globalisation and technocratisation of social work. *Critical Social Policy*, 16(2): 45–62.

Dunning, J. (2011) How bureaucracy is derailing personalisation. www.communitycare.co.uk (accessed 18 October 2011).

Ferguson, I. (2007) Increasing user choice or privatizing risk? The antinomies of personalization. *British Journal of Social Work*, 37: 387–403.

Glasby, J. and Duffy, S. (2007) *'Our Health, Our Care, Our Say': What Could the NHS Learn from Individual Budgets and Direct Payments?* Birmingham: Health Services Management Centre/In Control.

Glasby, J. and Littlechild, R. (2009) *Direct Payments and Personal Budgets: Putting Personalisation into Practice*, 2nd edn. Bristol: The Policy Press.

HM Government (2007) *Putting People First: A Shared Vision and Commitment to the Transformation of Adult Social Care*. London: Home Office.

Harris, J. and White, V. (eds) (2009) *Modernising Social Work*. Bristol: The Policy Press.

Horner, N. (2003) *What is Social Work? Context and Perspectives*. Exeter: Learning Matters.

Leadbeater, C. (2004) *Personalisation through Participation: A New Script for Public Services*. London: Demos.

Leece, J. and Leece, D. (2011) Personalisation: perceptions of the role of social work in a world of brokers and budgets. *British Journal of Social Work*, 41: 204–23.

O'Shea, B. (2011) Service User Perspectives, unpublished notes.

Parker, J. (2010) *Social Work Practice*, 3rd edn. Exeter: Learning Matters.

Putting People First consortium (2010) *The future of social work in adult social services in England: Statement*. London: Putting People First consortium.

Scourfield, P. (2008) Going for brokerage: a task of 'independent support' or social work? *British Journal of Social Work*, 40: 858–77.

Social Work Reform Board www.communitycare.co.uk/socialworkreformboard.

Waters, J. and Duffy, S. (2007) *Individual Budgets: Report on Individual Budget Integration*. www.in-control.org.uk (accessed 22 October 2011).

4

Personalisation and safeguarding

Introduction

This chapter will explore the direct association of safeguarding with personalisation and how this can have a direct influence upon the lives of individuals who are eligible for social care support. As we already explored in previous chapters, adults may become eligible for personal support due to a vast range of physical, social and environmental reasons and particular needs ranging from learning disability, physical disability, mental health and physical health problems or old age. It is often a combination of these factors and environmental influences such as poor housing, lack of social networks, inability to work and exclusion from mainstream society, which can compound and create layers of dependency leading to the need for social care referral, assessment and intervention. This layered dependency and exposure to heightened risks in day to day living can lead to vulnerability of exploitation and subsequent abuse.

Learning objectives for the chapter

1   To provide a historical and ideological context to the time line of adult safeguarding and the links with personalisation
2   To explore the links between adult vulnerability, risk of harm and exploitation and how this can lead to abuse and the factors that can cause this
3   To consider the impact of personalisation and safeguarding issues for family carers and relatives
4   To explore the diversity of individual experiences of personalisation by introducing three different service user scenarios
5   To develop practice experience of safeguarding and personalisation through reference to theory, legislation and social work models

The context of safeguarding and personalisation

Society has developed different ways of protecting people from abuse over the years. Until relatively recent times in the time line of history, people deemed to be unable to sustain ordinary lives were 'warehoused' away from their community to live in large institutions. The movement to re-settle people in the community and out of long stay hospitals has been a long journey triggered by influences such as the 1948 National Assistance Act, which initiated a significant transition from a national medical model of care for vulnerable adults towards a social model of support. Another influence came from America in the 1960s stemming from the strength of the disability rights movement and changes in ideological thinking about the importance of basic human rights for everyone, regardless of their disability. More recently, the NHS and Community Care Act (1990) was an important influence in the evolution of a 'needs led' rather than 'service led' response to supporting people. The disabled writer and activist Simon Heng has written about a 'New Victorian Era' in contemporary Britain (Heng 2010), caused by the current economic recession and the Government's rapid transformation of adult social care. Heng refers to the risks of a reduction in eligibility to welfare benefits, access to public services and assessed social care support. The idea of the Victorian division between the 'deserving' and the 'undeserving' poor and the subsequent reward of charitable help for those deserving of this support, while others ended up in workhouses, is a fear he refers to, particularly with regard to those who may have an invisible disability and are therefore more likely to lose benefits and those with a visible, clearly recognised need. Certainly, issues around the help and support offered to people have changed over time, yet there appears to be a tendency to cyclical shifts in the ways that people with higher needs are supported in times of uncertainty, and as a result of the fast pace of change instigated through economic and political transformations.

Reflective exercise 4.1

- When considering risks to adults is there a 'hierarchy of need' which should be taken in to account before a service is provided?
- What ethical dilemmas do you think there may be in deciding the eligibility for support for one person as compared to another?

Heng refers to adults with invisible disabilities as often seeming less eligible for direct support than perhaps a person using a wheelchair. Kemshall (2002) argues that notions of risk and vulnerability are socially constructed and can lead to the targeting of resources for those considered to be of highest need. Beck (1992) refers to a 'risk society' where perceived and potential hazards within contemporary society are flagged up as needing to be minimised or avoided.

The increased focus on risk when determining the level of support to be provided can create tensions when deciding who needs protection through risk avoidance. An example of this is referred to by Shakespeare et al. (2006) who note that learning disabled adults are often considered by society to be 'at risk' of sexual exploitation due to widely held ideas about asexuality, vulnerability and innocence.

These concerns have been raised as an introduction as a way of steering forward an emphasis on safeguarding issues directly associated with personalisation, due to people's vulnerability to increased exposure to risks and how this can escalate to harm, abuse and exploitation. As a way of presenting these issues in a clear and pragmatic way we will focus on three very different individuals and how their lives have been altered by different circumstances due to a combination of factors causing them to become vulnerable and need social care support. The insight into individual lives will emphasise the complexities of personalisation and how the right intervention from social work/social carers can make a significant difference to outcomes for people and their families. Each case study will also explore the involvement of social workers and other health and social care professionals and will reflect on the lessons learnt from the intervention and different theory, legislation and perspectives which have a bearing on the scenarios.

An important aspect of safeguarding to stress before the life stories unfold, is the often complex intertwining of the lives of the vulnerable adult and their relatives/main carers. This interdependency of the carer and the person being cared for has become an increasing feature of personalised support. The 'Putting People First' (DH 1997) government transformation of adult social care has instigated staggering changes to how social care is being organized. It is forecast that the adult social care workforce could almost double between now and 2030 from 1.75 million to 3.1 million (Skills for Care' State of the Adult Social Care Workforce 2010 report). This would in effect mean that the social care sector will need 900,000 personal assistants to enable everyone who wishes to have a publicly-funded personalised budget and to remain in their own home. Safeguarding can be perceived as being a mammoth task, encompassing not only the protection of the person eligible for support, but also the personal carer, and the family carer, who may have experienced significant life changes in order to enable their relative to remain at home.

The following three case studies are based on real situations but all names, places and personal circumstances have been changed.

CASE STUDY 4.1

Violet Browning is 85 years old and lives in her own home in a small town with her husband, who is her main carer. Violet has dementia, which was diagnosed two years ago, and the symptoms have become slowly but progressively worse causing her to feel confused, prone to panic attacks and unable to carry out personal care or to be left unattended for longer that short periods of time. Violet also has some additional health problems caused by arthritis and asthma. Her husband William is 82 years old and has coped well in his caring role until recently, when he strained his back due to lifting Violet following a fall. William has become frail and anxious and has bouts of depression where he feels unable to cope any more. During a weekly shopping trip to the local supermarket with William, Violet wandered off and left the shop, wandering into the busy town centre. William called the police straight away. Violet was found an hour later on a side street, having been hit by a passing car and suffering from mild concussion and minor head and neck injuries. Violet was admitted to the local general hospital where she was seen and assessed by a hospital social worker. The social worker was aware of the need for Violet to be treated for the concussion and minor injuries caused by the accident and to give her time to recuperate from the emotional trauma of the incident. She was also aware that Violet would need rehabilitation if she was to return home, rather than be admitted to a residential service and that both Violet and William wanted to avoid the option of long term care. However, during a conversation with William following an afternoon visit to the hospital, concerns were raised, as William confided that he had resorted to locking his wife in her bedroom at night and restraining her in her chair to avoid her wandering into the kitchen and turning on the gas cooker.

Questions to consider

This case study throws up dilemmas which may be frequently experienced by many older people and their relatives in modern day life. There are questions to reflect on:

1   What risk factors culminated in the crisis for both Violet and William and how could this situation have been avoided?

2   What immediate priorities need considering to support both the service user and the carer?

3   How can the professionals and the different agencies involved work together to ensure a positive outcome for Violet and William?

4   How can personalised support be used most effectively to reduce the risks and enable Violet to return home safely?

Issues arising

Dementia is an increasing health condition for large numbers of people in Britain. This has been escalated by the rising number of people who are living longer and an increase in the early diagnosis of dementia. This has resulted in a significant pressure on health and social care resources and an increased demand for personalised support to retain people in their own homes. There are some particular issues within this case study, which can be explored further and which also reflect on the questions raised:

Age and ageism

Violet and William became vulnerable in their home due to a culmination of factors, which were partly caused by their advancing age. This was clearly exacerbated by Violet's dementia and William's inability to cope with the emotional burden of his caring role. An issue of central importance here concerns the ingrained ideas in society about age and ageism and the tendency for professionals to make assumptions about older people's capacity to have a say about the life choices available to them. Research carried out by the Joseph Rowntree Foundation in 2009 found that older people's voices are 'subdued' in care planning and many of their views are represented through other people's experiences, rather than their own. The study identified that, although there is a dramatic move to provide personalised care and support in people's own homes, there is not a similar drive to support older people to participate in this change of care culture. This can result in older service users who 'continue to be perceived as passive recipients of care first and foremost' (Bowers 2009: 36). It may be that Violet's voice is subsumed with the concerns of both her husband and the professionals who may have made important life changing decisions on her behalf. Violet's dementia may extend the feelings of powerlessness due to feeling confused and her limited capacity to make decisions and feel in control of things. In terms of the implications for abuse in this context, the implicit discrimination experienced by older people who do not have a voice may result in risks of a gradual and escalating loss of personal control and identity and vulnerability to feelings of marginalisation and possible exploitation.

Medical and social models of care

Violet and William's basic and immediate needs may be interpreted differently, according to the type of care and professional help being provided. The hospital environment will be organised within the regime of a medical model of care. The biological or physiological approach to illness, old age and disability begins from the perspective that the circumstances of someone's life result directly from the physical impairment and individual health needs (Parker and Bradley 2007). The medical model for dementia could result in medication or medical treatments that aim to cure the behaviours. 'Because there is no cure for dementia, the medical model is a pessimistic one' (Marshall and Tibbs 2006: 6). Within the hospital setting, therefore, Violet's medical diagnosis may be reductionist in perspective and dwell on the notion that it is impossible to communicate with a person with dementia. There may be a real tension here for hospital social work intervention, as the social work code of practice will be based primarily on the social model. The social model recognises that society puts up barriers that disable the older person, such as poor access and transportation or less tangible attitudes and values towards people, which are discriminatory and judgmental. Vernon (2002) also raises the point that multi-oppressions can be created by application of the medical model; in Violet's case this may link to her age, gender and ill health. The medical model within a hospital setting can give rise to institutional practices which are not able to provide the time and attention needed for a person with complex needs. Mandelstam refers to institutional abuse as arising from poor practices which become 'accepted to the point, where it is considered no longer remarkable and certainly not a cause for formal concern' (Mandelstam 2009: 27). He refers to the situation where hospital social workers feel powerless to raise issues about dignity, nutrition, hygiene and continence within acute settings because they are part of the culture and a result of limited time and physical resources. When reflecting on the priorities for Violet, these may well be dictated by the treatment model of repairing physical injuries and not prioritising the emotional needs which may be equally important.

The interdependency of the service user and the carer

The dilemma of meeting William, the carer's, needs and responding to Violet's issues, even though both aspire to be able to return home, can be challenging and create tensions which need resolution. Kittay (1999) explores the interdependence between the carer and the vulnerable adult which can lead to an unequal distribution of power within the relationship. Shakespeare (2006) refers to the need to move away from the dependency cycle of the carer and the service user towards 'interdependency' and power sharing. Power inequalities within a relationship can stem from the dependency of one person upon another within a care giving/care receiving relationship. In this scenario it could be seen that Violet will become increasingly dependent upon her husband as the key carer, which may well put increased pressure on their relationship. There is also the increasing concern about William's health and well-being, who may also be perceived as a vulnerable adult in need of support. The mental ill health he is experiencing may be reactive and may increase due to his wife being taken into hospital and subsequent concerns about their future and how he will cope if Violet returns home.

Risk taking models

There may also be tensions between the duty of care to protect a vulnerable person within a 'safety first' notion of risk and the notion that risk should be 'owned' by the person who is seen to be vulnerable. The service user may well be able to contribute to decisions about their own lives, even if others perceive the decisions as unwise (Titterton 2006). In this scenario Violet and William may both aspire to return home and resume the support plan with increased personal assistance from an individual budget capable of providing the support needed. The dilemma of increasing quality of life conditions may well also increase the risks of increased exposure to harm, vulnerability and the day to day hazards of ordinary life. However, this needs to be carefully weighed up and balanced to look at the strengths and abilities of the person and the acceptable level of risk that can be taken. Stevenson (1999) suggests that we need to consider the interaction between the need and the risk, to ensure that any review of needs takes into account an agreed level of risk taking. In the scenario, it can be assumed that an increased risk factor would be balanced out by the increased quality of life for Violet and William if they are able to return to their home.

Deprivation of liberty

There are also factors to consider which will fall in to the remit of 'Deprivation of Liberty' detailed within the Mental Capacity Act (2005). Section 5 of the Act provides a general defence for people providing care or treatment for a person lacking capacity, if it is considered to be in their best interest. William had made an assumption that Violet lacked capacity to be safe within the home without 24 hour supervision. His response to ensuring her safety was to secure her to a chair to prevent her from getting to high risk places in the home, such as the kitchen or leaving from the front or back doors. This is unlikely to be assessed as a case of wilful neglect or intended abuse, because William is struggling to sustain the best interests of his wife within a very distressing situation. This scenario reflects the ethical dilemmas of caring for an older, frail person at home when the carer also needs help to cope. The social work role in this situation would be to support the carer and to put certain safeguards in place before Violet can be returned home. This may mean that 24 hour support would need to be provided to ensure that the risks of harm to Violet and deprivation to her personal liberty are removed.

Social work intervention

The questions to reflect on and the key issues arising are now followed up with a summary of the social work involvement following Violet's accident and subsequent admission to hospital.

The social worker met with both Violet and her husband on the first day of hospital admission and liaised with the medical staff to record the initial treatment that Violet would require following the accident. A week later the social worker carried out a Community Care Assessment prior to hospital discharge assessment and agreement. A Carer's Assessment was also carried out with William. A referral was made to an independent living service geared to providing person centred support and clinical intervention to people in hospital who are preparing to return to the community. This is a joint health and social care funded initiative where personalised support is provided in a person's own home. Social care staff provide the support, but are trained to be able to provide personal care, administer medication and carry out clinical interventions.

The social worker had knowledge of other organisations and resources and was able to look creatively at ways in which Violet could be cared for at home. Pressures to move Violet from hospital before becoming overdependent and the pressure of bed blocking were motivators to quick thinking and action.

The views of the patient and the carer were taken on board and risk assessments were person centred. Central to the ethos of personalisation are the social work values which have consistently promoted putting the person first; values such as respect for the individual and self-determination are influencing factors. The British Association of Social Workers (BASW) states that social work is committed to five basic values of human dignity and worth; social justice; service to humanity; integrity; and competence (BASW 2002).

Social work intervention in this particular situation would be focused on getting the right solution for both the person with dementia requiring social support and also for the carer. When analysing how a professional worker manages to 'think on their feet' to problem solve a complex and multilayered dilemma it is helpful to 'unpack' how this process of 'Reflection in Action' actually takes place (Schön 1983). It is recognised that social work and other professions where vulnerable people are in turmoil and need help and support are very complex jobs. Pam Trevithick has written about the knowledge base of social work as a way of understanding that social work practice is a highly skilled activity requiring a diverse and extensive knowledge base. Trevithick explores the knowledge framework and separates out three distinct domains of knowledge: theoretical knowledge, factual knowledge and practice knowledge (Trevithick 2008). In this particular case, the social worker would need to have theoretical knowledge of different approaches and methods such as procedures to assess and implement the social work task. It would also be necessary to have factual knowledge about specific legislation and policy procedures, such as the Mental Capacity

Act (2005) and also would require practice knowledge, which includes the personal knowledge the social worker has built up about the service user and carer's lives.

Lessons to learn

It is often after a crisis that reflection on the action can reveal alternative or additional interventions which may have alleviated or removed some of the stress and severity of the incident. What lessons could have been learnt from the issues emerging from this case study?

1   Violet could have been eligible for a mental capacity assessment to ascertain what areas of her life she could still have capacity to make decisions about. As stressed in the Mental Capacity Act (2005) an essential feature of capacity assessment is to ensure that judgements are not made about the quality of the decision being made by the person who may have limited capacity due to illness or disability. Another key feature to consider is that any intervention necessary must be as non-invasive as possible, and respectful of the person's right to a good quality of life.

2   William may need practical and emotional support to work through possible feelings of guilt about his coping strategy in keeping Violet safe. Social work intervention would need to monitor how William as the main carer is coping, and the impact of his mental health on his confidence to return to his caring role. This will be an important factor in ensuring that Violet's rights as a human being are not infringed by deprivation of liberty issues.

CASE STUDY 4.2

Peter Jackson is 32 years old and lives in a rural market town in a flat owned by the district council as part of the social housing stock. Peter has a moderate learning disability linked with cerebral palsy and some associated sight and mobility impairments. Ten years ago Peter lived with his parents and three brothers in a small town nearby. He attended a local day service for three days a week and also used the local swimming and leisure centre most evenings. Peter was one of the first service users in the county to be offered a direct payment following the Direct Payments Act in 1996. His life changed quickly, from living in the family home to moving into his own home and gaining ten hours a week personal support from a social care worker supplied by a local domiciliary agency. Peter was able to identify what help he needed and how he wanted to use his funding. He was able to attend a local adult education class in woodwork and decorating skills for three mornings a week and start some voluntary work which would lead to paid employment at a nearby hardware store. Peter became well known in the local area and began to call into his local pub two or three evenings a week. He was befriended there by a group of young men who offered him cigarettes and free drinks. Within three months the relationship had become exploitative, with two of the men visiting Peter at his home at all hours of the day and night. The flat became the base for them to meet girlfriends and store stolen goods. Peter was threatened to keep quiet or be reported to the police for 'doing bad things'. This evolving situation coincided with a re-assessment of Peter's personal budget, which reduced the personal support plan from ten to six hours a week. During this three month period Peter lost weight, as his food was being eaten by others and he was subjected to physical abuse from the two men in the form of kicking and spitting and also emotional abuse through constant ridicule and threats of further violence. Peter's personal assistant, who now only visited on three mornings every week, became concerned due to Peter's weight loss and subdued behaviour and reported her concerns to the local community team. A social worker was identified within the team to do a home visit.

Questions to consider

The experience of this young man who has moderate learning and physical disabilities and is living in his own home in the community is an increasingly familiar feature of modern day life. There are questions to consider arising from this case about the increase of discriminatory abuse and the impact this can have on the person being abused.

1   How did this situation escalate into a crisis when members of the public, local agencies and the social work team should have been alerted to initial warning signs that something was wrong with Peter?

2   What support could have been put in place for the personal assistant to ensure that a safety net of resources was put in place to avoid risk of exploitation?

3   Why are people with disabilities still a target for discrimination and abuse in society and how can this be prevented?

4   What support needs to be put in place to help Peter recover from his ordeal and retain his independence, yet be protected from risk of harm and exploitation?

Issues arising

The features identified in this case study have, sadly, been captured in numerous real life experiences for vulnerable adults in the community who are perceived as easy targets for victimisation and abuse. The following factors have been identified to respond to the questions raised and build on knowledge of the circumstances for Peter and how to limit or eliminate the potential for abuse.

Eligibility for support

A key issue for Peter is the re-assessment of his eligibility for personal support. Peter had been re-assessed within the last six months of being issued with a direct payment resulting in reduced hours and a lowering of the support network needed to ensure his safety and well-being. There has been a recent national review of eligibility criteria and reduced resources for social care funding. A focus on the risks linked with choice and independence is stressed within the 'Fair Access to Care Services' (DH 2003) guidance. In England, local authorities follow central government guidance on thresholds and fair levels of access to care and support and need to 'assess people's needs in terms of risks to their independence' (Mandelstam 2009: 151). The empowering and life changing capacity of personalised support may have a negative edge if support hours are reduced thereby extending the scope for exploitation and the reduction of the safety net of support. As stated by Mandelstam, 'the setting of thresholds means that not all needs or risks will be met' (Mandelstam 2009: 151).

The tragedy model of disability

Peter is an example of an increasing number of adults with learning disabilities who are now living with support in the community. However, the transformation from residential care to supported living has been hampered by the sustained and ingrained ideas often held by people in society about disability. The tragedy model (Swain and French 2008) links people's ideas about disability with the biological or medical model of disability which portrays disability as 'a deficit, a personal burden and a tragedy' (Wilder 2006: 2). The tragedy model has its roots within the medical model. The labelling of people who may have visible and multiple disabilities may also influence their status in society, linked to the extent to which they are able contribute to society. There has recently been a significant increase in the media coverage of discriminatory abuse and exploitation of people with learning disabilities who have been harassed, bullied, abused and even murdered by members of the public and relatives. An example of this was the media coverage of Steven Hoskins. He was a 39-year-old man with a learning disability who was emotionally, physically and financially abused in his own home. He was then forced to jump from a viaduct by his three persecutors and dropped to his death. This tragic case was influenced by a lack of communication between many agencies who knew Steven, including social workers, police, store detectives and the local hospital. Peter would have been perceived as a vulnerable person who could be exposed to exploitation, yet this was not picked up on by local people who knew him.

Perceptions of power

Personalisation may have indirectly caused an increase in discriminatory abuse due to the visibility in the community of disabled people living ordinary lives, rather than set apart from society in institutions. The discrimination experienced by disabled people may be partly due to the perceived power imbalance between disabled and non-disabled people. The French philosopher Michel Foucault developed ideas about power and its central role in 'The Order of Things'. Foucault made a distinction between power dominating people, and knowledge or truth setting people free. He saw power as transcending across generations and linked to layers of oppression and structural ideas about who holds the power in society. When considering the rise of personalisation as an alternative to the Welfare State from a structural and political perspective, it could be that the government's policy of stepping back and promoting increased control for the individual, the family unit and local community could decrease equality of opportunity. From a personal perspective, Peter has been directly affected by a reduction in his personal budget which has had an impact on the level of risk he has been exposed to. From a cultural angle it can also be seen that local services and agencies supporting Peter need to be able to recognise their skills and resources to work together effectively to enable vulnerable individuals to live safely as part of their community.

'The Big Society'

The reduction in the involvement of statutory provision and the State's increasing tendency to take more of a backwards step from providing direct services has had a strong impact on the shape of adult social care support. 'The Big Society' is a feature of personalisation promoted by the government as a shift from public dependency on delivering services towards the individual, their family and local private and voluntary groups taking more control of vulnerable members of the community. 'The Big Society' does need to embrace the ideas and views of disabled people, and to listen to the support they feel they need from their local community. This view would be favoured by the disabled activist and academic Vic Finkelstein, who argued that the study of culture is crucial to the development of disability studies: 'It is vital that all disabled people join together in their own organisation so that there is a creative inter-action . . . It is this interaction that can be particularly fruitful in helping us to take the initiative in developing a new disability culture' (Finkelstein, quoted in Campbell and Oliver 1996: 111–12). Here, the importance of self-advocacy is promoted. With reference to Peter's experiences it will be important to listen to his perspective on what has happened and ensure that his thoughts, views and plans for the future are central to any professional intervention.

Adult safeguarding legislation

It could be argued that there is a real need for an increase in legislative powers to strengthen the adult safeguarding procedures and practices across all local authorities. Peter may have had more immediate and direct intervention if there was a more rigorous adult safeguarding procedure available to him. Following the political change to a coalition government there has been a delay in updating 'No Secrets' (DH 2000). Mandelstam recommends the need to make mandatory the definitions of what constitutes abuse, that there needs to be a statutory obligation to have adult safeguarding boards in every local authority, clear inter-agency partnerships and defined roles and responsibilities (Mandelstam 2009). An important aspect of the recommendations of the 'No Secret's Review' is the duty of professionals to act and cooperate when abuse allegations are suspected or reported. A local authority appeal against payment of compensation to victims of abuse was overturned due to the lack of a legal, general duty of protection on the local authority of Hounslow in 2008. This was the case of Hounslow X and Y; two adults with learning disabilities who were harassed and abused by a group of young people in their own home (Naylor 2006). The legal position for Peter as a victim of abuse needs to be considered as he may be eligible for compensation. However, there are variable factors here, such as the local authority, position on how Peter was supported and the loop holes within adult safeguarding legislation which may go against the payment of financial compensation.

Multiple layering of disability

Vulnerability in terms of a person with learning disabilities can also be compounded by the higher rates of physical and mental ill health experienced by people with learning disabilities. In Peter's case, he has a physical and a learning disability and also mental health issues due to the exposure to abuse. There can be further problems created for people with multiple disabilities due to the poor access to mainstream health services. Valuing People Now (DH 2009) identified the slow pace of progress with improving health access for people with learning disabilities and the Mencap report 'Death by Indifference' (Mencap 2007) highlighted the cases of six people who were claimed to have died needlessly and suffered pain and lengthy bouts of ill health because their initial health issues were not dealt with efficiently and effectively. Mencap referred to the treatment as 'institutional discrimination' against people with learning disabilities (Parker 2010: 57). Peter will have health related needs following on from the abuse he has suffered which need the right level of support. It will be important to ensure that he is supported to communicate these to medical staff in his preferred style of communication.

Social work intervention

The following summary identifies what action was taken by the community social work team and the gaps in their intervention which may have led to the severity of the outcome for Peter.

Peter was well known to the local community team and has had regular reviews and risk assessments; the last one resulting in a drastic reduction in his funded support hours from ten hours a week to two hourly drop in calls three times a week. As Peter had no contact from his family, due to his parents dying and his brothers taking posts in the army abroad, he became more reliant on local networks of support. When the community team were alerted to the suspected abuse a social worker was allocated and an investigation set up with the local Safeguarding Vulnerable Adults Board. Allegations of physical, emotional and financial abuse were investigated. The investigated involved a local police safeguarding officer, the local health centre and the domiciliary agency providing weekly support for Peter. The two young men were arrested and sentenced to 12 months imprisonment due to intent to deceive and the infliction of grievous bodily harm.

Peter was re-located to a flat linked up to 24 hour support through telecommunication. This comprised of a telephone link service to the domiciliary agency. Due to some health issues and reduced confidence in living independently following the abuse incidents, Peter was re-assessed as critical need, his support hours increased and risk reducing initiatives were put in place including a health passport and a person centred plan. The health passport and personal plan were set up by Peter with support from the social worker and personal assistant to clearly record his health needs, regular health appointments, key people to contact, likes, dislikes and other necessary information for Peter to share with professionals and agencies if required. These user-friendly documents were owned by Peter to take with him to health appointments or review meetings.

Lessons to learn

The case study really identifies the central importance of communication and of picking up on cues indicating that a person may be at risk before this has a chance to escalate towards an abusive situation. (Koprowska 2010). In hindsight, the following factors could have alleviated or prevented this escalation of events.

1   Good inter-agency working could have prevented things developing in to discriminatory abuse. A pragmatic interpretation of 'The Big Society' could be encouraging local citizens to 'look out' for vulnerable members of the community. For example, local users of the pub used by Peter could keep an eye open for any exploitative behaviours and be encouraged to report any concerns to the community police or social work teams.

2   Also worth considering would be a simplification of the adult safeguarding investigation process. The Association of Directors of Social Services (ADASS 2005) recommended an eight step procedure for handling adult safeguarding cases. The stages include alerts of possible abuse, deciding whether a safeguarding enquiry is necessary, formulating a plan for assessing risk, carrying out the assessment, drawing up a plan to tackle any identified risks, reviewing the plan and recording any outcomes. This process could be further simplified to ensure that a personalised approach is used to ensure that the process is manageable. For example, local authorities in London have condensed their safeguarding procedures down to four basic stages: alert, strategy, case conference and review. Less cumbersome intervention could have resulted in a quicker response towards meeting Peter's need for help.

3   The care management model of social work may not always be fully effective in picking up on the early signs of abuse, due to the heavy emphasis on data based case work and limited time free for preventative, community based social work. A central part of personalisation is the introduction of the support brokerage model. This could be perceived as an alternative, more preventative model of social work practice in working with vulnerable adults. Within the support brokerage model of social care, the social worker would be seen as a central person to work with support brokerage to signpost service users and carers to local services. The role could include providing information, advice and technical assistance to develop, cost out, negotiate implement and mediate plans as required by the individual. This conjures up an idea of a more 'hands on' proactive and preventative approach to social work, which is not bound into the managerial care management approach to social work assessment and intervention.

4   Also relevant here is how the service user and carer understand the change from traditional service support to a personalised approach, as opposed to the political promotion of the ethos of personalisation. A study carried out to interview people

with learning disabilities in order to find out their direct experiences of personal support showed that their understanding was rooted in the 'hands on' support they received. The highest value was placed on the helping relationship itself and the circle of support available to the person receiving personal support (Sowerby 2010). The direct experiences of disabled people; how they understood personalisation in terms of their own life and the practical ways that support had enabled independence were considered most important to those interviewed. With reference to Peter's case, more could have been done to help him to look out for signs of abuse, to understand the situations to avoid and to know what to do and who to contact if he felt threatened in any way. Social workers have an important role to play in believing that people can make positive changes in their lives if they are given the support and the resources to make this happen.

5   Practical solutions to keeping vulnerable people safe can be quite simple but very effective. For example, some London authorities have plans in place to introduce a pre-payment card for those people who receive personal budgets. Council funding can be transferred on to the card and this would then be used to pay for the support required. There would also be an audit trail to enable intervention if this is needed due to finances going astray. This preventative measure would protect the service user and act as a deterrent to the potential abuser.

CASE STUDY 4.3

Edher is 52 years old. Edher moved from Turkey to England six months ago to join his son, who married an English woman and set up a family catering business in London the previous year. Edher's wife had died soon after their only son married and left Turkey, leaving him alone and without a reason to remain in the small Turkish village. Edher had recently developed a number of physical and mental health problems, including diabetes, sight impairment, stomach ulcers and depression triggered by his bereavement, and had applied for disability benefits before moving to England. On arrival at Heathrow airport and ringing for a lift to his son's home, Edher discovered from his daughter-in-law that his son had been detained in prison due to family business disputes, allegations of theft and debts to local companies. His daughter-in-law was unable to help due to the full responsibility of the failing business and child care responsibilities. She did however, ring the social services office for the Heathrow area of London. Edher was stranded with nowhere to live, very little money, no understanding of the English language and no other contacts to seek help from.

After waiting for two hours Edher was approached by a social work assistant who had arrived with a member of the asylum support team, also located in the same office. After a brief meeting over a coffee in the airport cafeteria it was decided that the priority would be to set up respite accommodation for Edher as near to his son's family as possible, arrange for meals to be delivered and apply for disability benefits to be paid through the temporary address. Edher was confused and upset due to the sudden change of plans and uncertainty about his future; 'They called a cab and they sent me here to live. The council gave the address to the mini cab driver and they brought me here. They didn't tell me where I was going . . . . nothing. They used to give me frozen food . . . ready meal for six to eight months. After that is made me sick. I am still suffering now with that food. They sent me enough for a month or 20 days and they put it in the freezer here and each day they gave me two packs . . . believe me that made me sick' (Roberts 2002: 17).

Questions to consider

The situation Edher found himself in will be experienced by other people arriving in the UK to discover a sudden change in their circumstances, which may cause them to feel isolated, lonely and helpless. It could be argued that this lack of respect and dignity afforded to a vulnerable person by support agencies is a form of institutional abuse (Mandelstam 2009). There are issues here about the person's rights as a citizen to access the medical, social and personal support they are entitled to and some key questions to ponder on:

1   Why was Edher left to cope with minimal help, when his emotional, financial and physical need for assistance was critical?
2   What immediate assistance could Edher have benefitted from to avoid the escalation of disadvantage experienced?
3   How could the professionals and agencies have worked together more effectively to set up a support plan and network of resources for Edher?

Issues arising

There are some themes that arise from the experiences of Edher and the questions raised, which we can reflect upon:

The impact of multiple disability and loss

The layering of disadvantages caused by family loss, cultural and religious difference, physical and mental illnesses, poverty and language barriers have culminated to create significant vulnerability to risk, harm and exclusion. The impact of cultural change for Edher has perhaps provided the most powerful impetus to the increased vulnerability he has experienced in a new and unfamiliar environment. When experiencing a new culture there are signifiers to understanding the signs, symbols, tools and beliefs that are central to the social order (Riddell and Watson 2003). Oliver (1990; Oliver and Barnes 1996) writes about the existence of a set of beliefs in British society, which are the norms followed by society. Oliver and other writers on disability see these norms as used to oppress disabled people as part of the accepted cultural ideology. The layering of disadvantage for Edher may well reflect on his cultural identity and he may be seen by others as unable to function normally due to his range of loss, ill health and religious difference. This, in turn, can lead to issues of oppression and exclusion.

Inter-professional practice

Agencies which are not working together effectively provide a prominent feature of this case study. The Government's commitment to the transformation of adult social care relies heavily on the effectiveness of a 'whole systems' approach towards the promotion of the health and well-being of individuals within a society. The Government's comprehensive spending review in 2007 announced a social care reform grant of £520 million to be used over the following three years to roll out the personalisation agenda (Hafford-Letchfield 2009). At the heart of this funding is the need for health and social care partners to collaborate in the delivery of services and support to individuals. In this case study there was limited holistic partnership working between social services, housing, health and benefits advice to streamline the support offered to Edher, although there was a short term emergency package of support which was hastily pulled together. This did not stretch to the sustainability of the short term measures put in place to signpost Edher to community resources. Also there is a need for longer term planning to promote preventative interventions and build on these for ongoing support. There was also an absence of the self assessment element of meeting need, which is central to personalisation. The scenario also refers to the asylum support officer attending the initial meeting with the social work assistant. This makes an assumption that Edher is an asylum seeker, although he has entered the country with a legitimate passport and with relatives living in the UK.

Mental health and loneliness

Edher's recent bereavement and crisis on reaching the UK has escalated his mental and physical ill health. Recent research has made a strong correlation between mental illness bereavement and loss, lack of self-esteem, loneliness and exclusion. The Lonely Society (Griffin 2010) was written by the Mental Health Foundation. There is a strong link made between modern lifestyles, exclusion, loneliness and depression. The report stresses that the escalation of loneliness due to sudden life changes and crisis to become chronic loneliness can lead to negative behaviour, isolation and depression. Contributing authors to the report, Jacqueline Olds and Richard Schwarz state: 'Depression has become a catchall complaint from everyone from the stay-at-home mother who talks only to toddlers all day to the angry, unemployed man who feels like life has handed him a raw deal.'

Vulnerability to risk

The concept of the social construction of risk (Alaszewski 1998) makes a clear link between risk, the way risk is socially constructed due to rationing of resources, and issues of vulnerability. There are tensions between eligibility to social care support and the social model of support if the barriers within society are not being removed and vulnerable people are being left with inadequate levels of support. A central core of social work values is the importance of respecting and promoting the service user's right to self-determination. The delicate balance between rights and risks requires sensitive and measured professional judgement. Humphries argues that social work has moved from a concern with welfare to risk management and levels of dangerousness (Humphries 2004). Edher will have moved very quickly from a person with status in his own community to a person perceived to be 'needy' and at risk due to the limited support he has received.

The advocacy role

It could be argued that Edher also needed an advocate to support and speak up for him right at the beginning of his contact with professional services, due to the unexpected situation he was suddenly thrown into. Dominelli, a prominent social work academic, promotes the importance of challenging structural inequalities associated with race, gender, religion, class, culture, sexuality, ability and age. Dominelli argues that social work must advocate for social justice and to overtly challenge the welfare system: 'Valuing difference is one dimension to the complexities of life to be addressed explicitly by practitioners subscribing to anti-oppressive practice' (1988: 10)

Social work intervention

More experienced social work involvement came eventually, after four weeks of fragmented and poorly coordinated responses from an allocated social work assistant, housing agency, benefits agency and the local health service, where Edher was registered after moving into his temporary accommodation.

The social work assistant was supported by a more senior social worker, who contacted a local support broker dealing with personal support for people with mental health needs. Following a Community Care Assessment and a Self Assessment supported by an interpreter, an individual budget was agreed and was funded through a direct payment to Edher. He was also re-located after six months to a small apartment owned by a community housing association and gained tenancy entitlement. Edher was supported to employ his own personal assistant by the allocated support broker, who spent a period of two months with Edher and provided the practical advice and support necessary to set up a budget to manage the money and also to enable him to decide what support he needed to prioritise. Edher was able to resume contact with his son and family and use public transport for his weekly visits. Other support put in place was help to link up with social and religious groups in the area and regular health checks for his diabetes and stomach ulcer. Edher also joined a local support group for people who had experienced loss and had access to a counsellor to help him with his unresolved grief.

Lessons to learn

1   Early intervention and a well coordinated plan to put in all the practical, social and emotional support needed would have made a significant difference to Edher and his ability to cope with the chaos and anxiety he was experiencing. Social work is essentially about promoting social change and intervening at a time in a person's life when they are experiencing crisis and change and some degree of personal loss. In a three year national project supported by the Joseph Rowntree Foundation, Peter Beresford and colleagues (2007) asked 111 people who were either dying or had been bereaved what they most valued in palliative care social

workers. Three key factors emerged: the quality of the relationship with the social worker, the personal qualities of the social worker and the nature and process of the intervention. Edher's case may have lacked the personal touch that would have made all the difference, particularly during the early stages of intervention when short term measures were hastily put in place.

2   It is vital to listen to the person to fully understand the situation and ensure that their views, needs and preferences are of central importance. Deeper and enhanced levels of communication skills are essential for social work practice, particularly when there are differences in language and culture to overcome. Koprowska (2010) stresses the importance of removing the barriers people face when speaking a minority language and checking out the person's understanding to ensure that decisions are not arrived at without their full involvement. This would have been of real value for Edher to remove the communication barrier.

3   It is very important to combat the serious impact of loneliness and exclusion. Based on Bowlby's seminal work on loss, Kubler-Ross developed her work on the breaking of bad news and her 'five stages of grief'. (Kubler-Ross 2005). The five stages identified are described as: denial, anger, bargaining, depression and acceptance. Other writers have considered different theories; Stroebe and Schut (1995) developed ideas about coping with loss as being only one half of the spectrum, and that of equal importance in distancing from the loss and moving forward with life. Further emphasis on the importance of the emotional changes caused by crisis, loss and change could have been initiated in the early stages of intervention rather than as an added feature of the final support package for Edher.

Linked research

The following research identifies some ideas about social work which are informed by the integration of values, theories and social work models. These are common to all three case studies and draw out some of the material we have covered.

Value based practice

The central value base of social work is well grounded within Biestek's ethical principles (Biestek 1957):

- individualisation;
- purposeful expression of feelings;
- controlled emotional involvement;
- acceptance;
- non-judgemental attitude;
- confidentiality;
- client self determination.

Over fifty years later, there is still a good match between these traditional social work values and the introduction of personalised support which has the scope to liberate service users and practitioners, if the approach is creative and imaginative and geared to removing or reducing the defences of limited resources. It is recognised that working with the very vulnerable people in society will involve confronting exploitation and fraud and emotional and physical abuse. There is endless scope for abuse to happen when a system is individualised. Practitioners need support to be resilient and strategies to help them think about the task in hand and an imaginative approach to achieve this. Supervision is a central part of the support that professionals working on the front line need to provide the space to 'reflect on action' and gain support, guidance and advice about complex dilemmas in practice.

Theory base of practice

Social workers and other social care practitioners need knowledge and understanding of a 'tool kit' of theories and models which can often be used in an eclectic way to help us respond to personalisation and safeguarding issues. The three case studies provide scope to draw on a range of theory to enhance practice and to influence the ways that professionals intervene. Practice needs to comply with social work values, yet may vary greatly from one case to another, according to the predominating individual issues. A few different theories are listed here and are often used in a holistic way when working with individuals.

Task centred practice
This will focus on achievable outcomes which are identified by the service user. This has a clearer service user emphasis in personalised support and links with the importance of self assessment. The step by step approach of working with individuals encourages ownership and control away from the professional towards the person with the support needs.

Psychodynamic and person centred approaches
These stem from psychology and Carl Rogers' person centred counselling. The respect for human dignity and worth, integrity and capacity to reduce oppression and challenge the abuse of power are vital aspects of the social work skill base, as is the notion of 'unconditional, positive regard' and a non-judgemental approach. The service user's personal experiences of oppression and discrimination and what impact this has on them can be gleaned through enhanced communication skills and listening to people's own life stories.

Citizenship and co-production
The vulnerable adult with complex and multiple challenges due to disability, age, health or cultural differences may not be fully able to access their basic human rights as a citizen without support. The support brokerage model linked with personalisation provides a strong anchor for citizenship and co-production, where the service user is supported to be fully engaged and in control of the decisions being made about their life. Social workers need to be aware of what is out there in terms of grants and

funds from voluntary sector signposting to other resources, etc. The service user as an equal partner or co-producer should be seen as the expert, being given informed information about their entitlements and new ways to spend the allocated individual budget. Despite the risks associated with personalised support in people's own homes, there may be an important redress here, with the reduction in the numbers of people moving into residential and nursing homes. This may not only reduce the impact of institutional forms of abuse but also cut down on the number of deaths of older people after they move in to residential/nursing provision.

Social models of support and empowerment

Inclusiveness is the key aspect of personalisation and the importance of avoiding segregated services where possible. Labelling people as mentally ill, disabled or old is discriminatory and chips away at a person's identity. A point to reflect on is that only one in every 16 people in the population in the UK calls on social services help and many of these will be for a limited time. This can in itself be divisive and create a barrier between those that cope without social work support and those deemed to be vulnerable and needy. In contrast, other publicly funded services such as transport, education and health will be accessed by everyone during their life span. An empowerment model would be looking at what society has to offer each and every person and in turn, what each person has to offer to their society, rather than being viewed as on the receiving end of funding and support.

Chapter summary

We have explored the changing arena of adult social care and focused on the delicate balance between empowering people through personalised support and keeping them safe. The chapter has looked at some of the influences of the rich history of safeguarding vulnerable adults which has shaped and coloured contemporary social work practice and the personal experiences of service users and carers.

We have also reflected on the impact that personalised support has on individuals, their families and for social work and social care. The case studies have provided the vehicle for exploring how varied individual experiences of personal support and risk of harm and abuse can be and the importance of a fluid and creative response from social work practitioners. Safeguarding adults can be seen to be more than a set of procedures driven by routine and reference to policies. We have looked more broadly at some of the theory, legislation and creative analysis that underpins social work practice. In this way we have been able to stress the importance of social work theory and values as central to our social work practice.

References

ADASS (Association of Directors of Social Services) (2005) *Safeguarding Adults: A National Framework for Standards of Good Practice and Outcomes in Adult Protection Work*. London: ADSS.

Alaszewski, A. (1998) Risk in a modern society. In A. Alaszewski, L. Harrison and J. Manthorpe (eds) *Risk, Health and Welfare*. Buckingham: Open University Press.

BASW (2002) British Association of Social Workers; Key Principles

Beck, U. (1992) *Risk Society*. London: Sage.

Beresford, P. (2007) *The Changing Roles and Tasks of Social Work from Service User's Perspective: Shaping our Lives*. London: General Social Care Council.

Biestek, F. (1957) *The Casework Relationship*. London: Allen and Unwin.

Bowers, H. (2009) *Older People's Vision for Long Term Care*. York: J. Rowntree.

Campbell, J. and Oliver, M. (1996) *Disability Politics: Understanding our Past, Changing our Future*. London: Routldge.

DH (1997) *Putting People First*. London: Department of Health.

DH (Department of Health) (2000) *No Secrets*. London: Department of Health.

DH (2003) *Fair Access to Care Services. Guidance on Eligibility for Adult Social Care*. London: Department of Health.

DH (2009) *Valuing People Now*. London: HMSO.

Dominelli, L. (1988) *Anti-racist Social Work*. London: Macmillan.

Dominelli, L. (1998) Anti-oppressive practice in context. In R. Adams, L. Dominelli and M. Payne (eds) *Social Work: Themes, Issues and Critical Debates*. London: Macmillan.

Griffin, J. (2010) *The Lonely Society?* Mental Health Foundation.

Hafford-Letchfield, T. (2009) *Management and Organisations in Social Work*, 2nd edn. Exeter: Learning Matters.

Heng, S. (2010) Welcome to the New Victorian Britain. *Community Care*, 1827: 10.

Humphries, B. (2004) An unacceptable role for social work: implementing immigration policy. *British Journal of Social Work*, 34: 93–107.

Kemshall, H. (2002) *Risk, Social Policy and Welfare*. Buckingham: Open University Press.

Kittay, E. (1999) *Love's Labour: Essays on Women, Equality and Dependency*. London: Routledge.

Koprowska, J. (2010) *Communication and Interpersonal Skills in Social Work*, 3rd edn. Exeter: Learning Matters.

Kubler-Ross, E. (2005) *On Death and Dying*. London: Tavistock.

Mandelstam, M. (2009) *Safeguarding Vulnerable Adults*. London: Jessica Kingsley.

Marshall, M. and Tibbs, M. (2006) *Social Work and People with Dementia: Partnerships, Practice and Persistence*. Bristol: Policy Press.

Mencap (2007) *Death by Indifference*. London: Mencap 2007.

Naylor, L. (2006) Adult protection for community care/vulnerable adults. In K. Brown (ed.) *Vulnerable Adults and Community Care*. Exeter: Learning Matters.

Oliver, M. (1990) *The Politics of Disablement*. New York: St. Martin's Press.

Oliver, M. and Barnes, C. *Disabled People and Social Policy: From Exclusion to Inclusion*. London: Longman.

Parker, J. (2010) *Social Work Practice*, 2nd edn. Exeter: Learning Matters.

Parker, J. and Bradley, G. (2007) *Social Work Practice*, 2nd edn. Exeter: Learning Matters.

Riddell, S. and Watson, N. (2003) *Disability, Culture and Identity*. Essex: Pearson; Prentice Hall.

Roberts, K. and Maris, J. (2002) *Disabled Asylum Seekers: The Social Model of Disability and UK Government Policy and Legislation*. 'Disabled People in Refugee and Asylum-Seeking Communities in Britain', Findings: Joseph Rowntree Foundation.

Schön, D. (1983) *The Reflective Practitioner*. New York: Basic Books.

Shakespeare, T. (2006) *Disability Rights and Wrongs*. London: Routledge.

Sowerby, D. (2010) What sort of helping relationships are needed to make personalisation happen and how can organisations be developed to support this? *Journal of Social Work Practice*, 24(3): 269–83.

Stevenson, O. (1999) *Elder Protection in Residential Care: What can we Learn from Child Protection?* London: Department of Health.

Stroebe, M. and Schut, H. (1995) The dual process model of coping with loss. Paper presented at the International work group on death, dying and bereavement, Oxford, UK: 1995.

Swain, J. and French, S. (2008) *Disability on Equal Terms*. London: Sage.

Titterton, M. (2006) *Risk and Risk Taking in Health and Social Welfare*. London: Jessica Kingsley.

Trevithick, P. (2008) Re-visiting the knowledge base of social work: a framework for practice. *Journal of Social Work*, 38: 121–3.

Vernon, A. (2002) *Multiple Oppression and the Disabled People's Movement*. London: Routledge.

Wilder, E. (2006) *Wheeling and Dealing: Living with Spinal Cord Injury*. Nashville: Vanderbilt University Press.

5

Experiences of personalisation from service users and carers

Introduction

This chapter will be exploring the progress made in supporting people through personalisation and will capture this through the personal experiences of service users and carers. As we discovered when considering the value base of personalisation in Chapter 1, there are often tensions for service users, their relatives and practitioners when balancing preferences, rights and choices with factors such as risk of exploitation from others if vulnerable adults are not safeguarded effectively. In this chapter we will be looking in more depth at what personalised support really means for people and their family carers, to explore important issues such as choice, rights, independence and autonomy and how the new way of supporting people has really made a difference. The chapter will focus on the vast range of individual need encompassing the personalisation remit and the particular challenges of delivering personal support to those people with multiple and complex needs. The Individual Budgets pilot project evaluation in 2008 (IBSEN 2008) will be explored, as this identifies some of the differences in the experiences of service user groups and carers and the tensions between support for carers and the promotion of choice and control for disabled and older people. The following quote illustrates the individuality of people's experiences of self directed support and the sense of a journey which is just beginning in adjusting to new ways of working:

> I mean I still feel it is early days for me cause I am still learning and I've been finding it hard to accept what has happened to me and I do struggle. I do struggle being disabled . . . I've still got it in my head that I can still do everything that I used to do before. So you are still trying to do as much as you did before. I feel embarrassed having to get people in to do things, you know cause all my life I've never had anybody. I've always done everything myself.
>
> (Direct Payment user)

Learning objectives for the chapter

1   To explore different experiences of individuals who have gained their support via personal budgets to identify both the positive elements and the barriers that may be faced for people with a range of disabilities and for people with mental health needs and older people

2   To also acknowledge the impact of self directed support for family carers and relatives and their important role in facilitating personalisation

3   To consider some of the discrepancies about how personalisation is interpreted and provided, which can cause differences in the experiences for the individual on the receiving end of personal funding

4   To explore power differentials between professionals and service users, as individuals gain more control over their lives and also to consider the ethical dilemmas for social workers as gate keepers for public funding and eligibility for personal support

In Control; key building blocks for personalisation

The central focus of personalisation, which places emphasis on the service user's needs, is part of a rich history of human empowerment and personal rights within adult social care evolving from Community Care legislation in the 1990s and moving away from fitting people around available resources and services. Direct Payment legislation in 1996 was a move along the continuum of ensuring that the individual remains central to service planning and delivery. The In Control project was set up in 2003 as an organisation promoting the creation of individual budgets. Initially this was a small service which supported a small number of people with learning disabilities to move away from traditional service support to receiving their own direct payment for social care support. In Control has developed to become an influential organisation encompassing the progress made in the personalisation process. In 2007 In Control developed seven steps for personalised support plans which are still very widely used across different local authorities and independent agencies:

- What is important to you?
- What do you want to change or achieve?
- How will you spend the money?
- How will you use your individual budget?
- How will your support be managed?
- How will you stay in control of your life?
- What are you going to do to make this plan happen?

(In Control 2007)

The interface between the social worker and the service user within the personalised model of support has been termed the 'helping relationship' by Sowerby (2010). Sowerby uses the term 'a helping relationship' to differentiate it from more traditional roles such as carer and care manager and to reinforce the step forward needed by the practitioner to engage in a more creative and interactive role, which moves away from managing the care plan towards conducting or facilitating as part of the support planning process.

Reflective exercise 5.1

Consider what elements of your own life are the most important to you.

What help would you value from a social worker to ensure that support was provided to enable you to continue to have a good quality of life?

What skills and knowledge do you have as the person who understands their own needs and future aspirations?

Although it may be difficult to envisage needing the help of a social worker to plan your own life, you may have considered the type of help you might appreciate. This may include signposting to local services, costing out the support required, providing a link to other services and professionals who may need to be involved in a support plan and advice about employing a personal assistant if this is required. Perhaps most importantly of all the social worker may be the person who can listen to your concerns, priorities and identified need for support and advocate on your behalf to help with the practicalities of setting up an individual support plan.

As the person who has the knowledge of your own life and what is most important to you, perhaps you have reflected on exactly what you would need help with to continue to live as a citizen and for your rights and individuality to be upheld and respected.

The impact of personalisation on the social worker role

The self directed model of personalised support has altered the social work role to emphasise the initial assessment and allocation of resources and the monitoring role through liaison with key people involved in supporting the service user and carer. Although the process is person centred and affords a high degree of service user autonomy there have been concerns flagged up on behalf of, and indeed by, the social work profession. Michelle Lefevre (2005) senior lecturer at the University of Sussex, is concerned about the dilution of social work skills away from developing the longer term relationships with users and the coordinating role which was central to traditional care management. This view contrasts with those of Sowerby mentioned earlier, who advocates for the essential importance of the social work relationship with service users within the personalisation framework. Peter Beresford has researched this topic in 'The Shaping Our Lives, National User Network' (Beresford 2007) to highlight the experience and views of service users and carers as social work tasks have altered due to the personalisation agenda. Service users reported a need to move away from traditional models of assessment and towards independence, self assessment and the importance of qualities for social workers, such as warmth, trust, openness, honesty, reliability and good communication skills.

The following case study depicts a service user being supported by a social worker and a support worker to manage her own individual budget:

CASE STUDY 5.1

Magda is a single mother with two young children who has recently developed multiple sclerosis. Magda was a senior nurse in a busy intensive care department of the local hospital and understands the debilitating effects of the illness and the future prognosis. Magda had long standing social work support from a hospital social worker who was able to coordinate a number of professionals to visit the home and provide support. Magda valued her social worker's support, although the care plan was becoming hard to manage; as her needs became higher and her children's care more complex there were times of the day when Magda was at risk as health visitor, nurse and occupational therapist were unable to call when she needed them. Following a review of changing circumstances Magda was asked if she would like an individual budget. This would be combined funding from the Individual Living Fund and the local authority social care funds. With initial support from the social worker Magda was able to advertise for her own live-in carer and a personal assistant to offer support when required during the day. Magda did not require a broker to support her to set up a support plan and gradually the social worker was able to reduce her input, enabling Magda to take control of her individual budget with a 12 monthly review of the support plan.

In this scenario the social worker altered her role from a coordinator of the original care plan involving a number of different agencies and professionals to a less directive role in monitoring and reviewing the support plan at six monthly intervals and being available if needed to signpost or provide advice on resources and allowance entitlements.

Questions to consider

1 In what ways has the social worker's role shifted from a traditional care management model to the role required for self directed support?

2 Thinking of the ethos of person centred planning central to personalisation, what are the gains for Magda in shifting from a traditional care plan to a self directed support plan?

3 What are some of the new skills and qualities that will be important for the social worker to practise in her current social work role to ensure that the service user and family are safeguarded and empowered to remain in control of their support needs?

You may have initially summed up the gains for the service user as being substantial, whereas the social worker may have lost some of the previous direct contact with Magda, and have been left with a stronger emphasis on the assessing and reviewing responsibilities. However, there are subtle yet important qualities for the social work profession to extend, including the ability to negotiate and advocate, to be able to signpost and access resources when requested and to work closely with a large number of other professionals and services. The Social Work Reform Board (SWRB) has recognised the importance of emotional resilience for social workers, particularly during this time of massive change. The SWRB state that continuing professional development should enable social workers to 'become more confident, emotionally resilient and adaptable to the changing demands of social work'.

Individual experiences of personalisation: individual budget pilot

We will now consider the variety of ways that personalisation can be carried out, depending on a wide range of variables such as individual need, local resources, the capacity of the service user to manage his or her own budget, the type of self directed funding received and the support network available to the individual.

In October 2008 The National Evaluation of the Individual Budget Pilot Programme (IBSEN) was published. One year after the Department of Health 'Putting People first: A Shared Vision and Commitment to the Transformation of Adult Social Care' (DH 2007) the IBSEN report shed findings on the benefits and the initial problems discovered for those people receiving individual budgets. The research piloted individual budgets providing support for older people, disabled adults and adults with mental health problems eligible for publicly-funded social care. Almost 1000 people were interviewed about their experiences and the outcomes six months after being offered an individual budget. Interviews were held with service providers, commissioning managers staff and managers and with service users and carers, to gain a wide perspective of the advantages and any teething problems experienced. In summary, the following factors were identified:

- The comparative cost of providing an individual budget was similar to the cost involved if a traditional service was used.
- There were problems fulfilling the intention to merge different funding streams as part of the overall individual budget allocated. This was felt to be particularly problematic because NHS funding was not included.
- People receiving an individual budget were more likely to feel in control of their daily lives compared with those with conventional support.
- Satisfaction was highest amongst mental health service users and physically disabled people and was lowest amongst older people. Although people with learning disabilities were more likely to feel they had control over their daily lives, there were often extra pressures experienced by family carers, who needed to take a large role in managing how the money was used.
- Staff involved in the piloting of the first individual budgets encountered challenges, including establishing boundaries for how the money could be spent and also concerns about safeguarding vulnerable adults.

It is an interesting reflection that, a few years on from the pilot, many of these initial concerns and very obvious benefits still remain and different experiences of service user groups are still a factor. As expressed by an adult with a physical disability: 'I can choose my own respite facilities, checking them out first to make sure they meet my needs as a disabled person. I can control where I go and pay for it with the IB (individual budget) money. You are the best judge of your own needs – not a social worker.' A person requiring more guidance and support due to their disability may well need much higher levels of assistance to be able to enjoy the benefits of a personal budget.

A paper published by the *British Journal of Social Work* (Buckner and Yeandle 2011) explores some of the issues from the perspective of support carers which arose from the individual budgets pilot projects in 2005–2007. The concluding summary stresses the positive outcomes for carers and the increased quality of life and control afforded to the service user also having a positive benefit for the family carers. However, one area identified in the study was the discrepancy between the eligibility of carers to have an assessment of their own needs and the number of carers who actually received a carer's assessment or review. The 2004 Carers (Equal Opportunities) Act aimed to ensure that carers were made aware of their rights to this assessment. Furthermore, The Carer's Strategy 2008 committed £150 million to breaks and services for carers, which was not ring fenced and resulted in only 23 per cent of the funds being spent by 2009/10. The study found that carers were not always included in the service user's assessment in terms of the support they may need themselves. There was also concern raised about the management of the individual budget and the responsibility some carers were expected to take to manage the accounts on behalf of the individual. As mentioned by one carer who was asked if she was prepared to manage the individual budget for their relative: 'No, I couldn't because it's bad enough getting myself up and (laughs) working out what hours I'm working and who's going to look after (service user) and where he's going to be and telling the taxis where to drop them, no, I couldn't possibly do any more' (carer of learning disabled person, cited in Moran et al. 2011: 11). The research identified the importance of recognising and managing the individual differences between disabled and older people and their carers and the sensitive and delicate social work skills required to achieve support for carers without compromising the choice and control of service users.

Research carried out by Flynn (2006) identified some concerns in the employment of personal assistants by individual service users themselves, who felt vulnerable due to the difficulties they experienced employing their own staff. Flynn interviewed 16 people and discovered that half of those spoken to had experienced abuse or exploitation. This ranged from dishonesty, lack of trust, incompetency and abuse including physical, sexual, psychological and financial. As quoted by one of the recipients of personal assistance: 'Even though I can say what I want, it's scary to think what it's like for people who are totally dependent. They'd be walked all over given half a chance' (Moran et al. 2011: 37)

Life stories from individuals experiencing personalised support

The following case studies will explore three very different experiences of self directed support to highlight the positive and negative aspects for the user and carer and also to identify different ways that self directed funding can be provided.

CASE STUDY 5.2

Jamal is a 42-year-old man who lives in a large city with his wife and young son. Jamal was an art and design technology teacher at a large secondary school. He inherited an eye condition called aniridia which was passed down from his father's side of the family. His eyesight began to deteriorate in his early 20s when he became blind in one eye. By the time Jamal was 35 he was registered as blind, became unable to carry out the role at the school and sought early redundancy. At this time Jamal experienced a breakdown of confidence and became very depressed and reluctant to leave the house or become involved in parenting or help in the home. His GP referred him to the local authority social work team.

Jamal was assessed as eligible for an individual budget. This is a budget which may come from several places; in Jamal's case it was a combined budget of social services and 'supporting people' funding. He was allocated a social worker to carry out the initial assessment and assist with the self assessment. He was then introduced to a support broker from the local authority to provide help to work out a support plan which would be a clear plan of how the assessed budget allocation would be spent. The plan needed to have clear outcomes linked to Jamal's assessed needs.

Jamal was very clear about how he wanted to spend the money; he had discovered that the local college provided a course in learning Braille. He also wanted to invest in some specialist software for his computer to enable him to continue to work in some way in his chosen career of design technology. Jamal also wanted to use some of the budget on a personal assistant who would also carry out driving duties to enable him to begin to travel from home again.

The broker allocated to support Jamal had been employed as a day service support worker until very recently, but due to the reformation of adult social care the day service had closed and most of the staff team were re-trained as support brokers. Due to the vast difference in the new role the broker was unsure about the decisions being made by Jamal and questioned whether they were 'wise decisions'. This caused some tensions for Jamal and his family and the social worker was called on to intervene.

Jamal was able to move on to manage his own individual budget and used the funding to enable him to complete the course on Braille communication, to develop new design technology skills and to travel independently with the support of his personal assistant. Jamal went on to complete a peer brokerage course which enabled him to become a support broker for other adults requiring assistance. He was able to use his design skills to help peers to create their support plans as interactive documents which could be easily accessed and updated.

As mentioned in the case study, Jamal discovered support brokerage as a service to enable him to personalise the help he wanted to meet his life plans. From this experience he was able to use his own skills and experiences to become a peer broker to pass on his knowledge of self directed support to others. Duffy (2010) has developed a citizenship theory base around personalisation which recognises the importance of ensuring that each individual has the chance to be treated as an equal citizen regardless of their differences. The model of 'peer brokerage' meets the central objectives of citizenship theory and can be seen as an evolving idea of personalisation in action. The concept of peer brokerage builds on Leadbeater's work in 2004 when he defined personalisation in the following terms: 'putting users at the heart of services, enabling them to become participants in the design and delivery, services will be more effective by mobilising millions of people as co-producers of the public goods they value' (Leadbeater 2004: 255)

Reflective exercise 5.2

You may want to research peer brokerage as one of many brokerage models to find out what the practical aims and outcomes of peer brokerage are and why they would be relevant to this particular case study.

Question to consider

Why do you think Jamal's support broker was uncomfortable with his plans to use his individual budget?

The broker had transferred from a more structured and formal role within a group day service setting and may have found the transformation to a more autonomous and person centred role quite challenging. Legislation which is central as a guide for new brokers is the Mental Capacity Act (2005). The Mental Capacity Act stresses the importance of assuming capacity of a person to make a decision, even if it is considered to be 'unwise' by others. The decision-making process used to be within the domain of the social worker/carer role but now the emphasis is on the individual making their own mind up about life planning, while also taking into account risks that link to the specific choices made. This is a sensitive change which also needs to recognise that if a person is assessed as lacking capacity to make a decision about a certain aspect of their life, the social worker has a role to play to help a person to make decisions. This role is included within the Mental Capacity Act and is referred to as the 'best interest' decision-making process.

CASE STUDY 5.3

Hannah is a young woman aged 19 who has just left secondary education. Hannah has Down's Syndrome and some hearing impairment in her left ear. Hannah's parents are strong advocates for her rights as an individual and have maintained her in mainstream education and have had ongoing contact with the adult disability social work team to ensure that Hannah makes an effective transition from children to adult support.

The social worker has involved Hannah in the assessment process over the last three years to ensure that she is fully involved in her future plans. Hannah's person centred plan is based on Hannah's desire to have her own flat near to the family home. Hannah is allocated a personal budget; this is funding which comes directly from the local authority and can be managed by the authority on the person's behalf. The person and family must be told exactly how much money they have and be able to spend it in the way that makes sense to them, within the guidelines of ensuring that there are clear outcomes which are achievable. Hannah's mother is paid to provide personal assistance and a small flat is rented from a local housing agency. Hannah attends college three days a week and has a part time cleaning job at the local cafeteria.

Hannah adjusts surprisingly quickly to her new lifestyle. Her mother spends regular time with her during the week to support with areas of her life such as budgeting, shopping and cooking. Hannah tends to go home at weekends. Recently Hannah has wanted to spend more time away from her family and has developed a close relationship with an older man, who visits the flat regularly. Hannah's mother unexpectedly comes to the flat one evening and discovers them in bed together. Hannah's parents are upset and angry and call the social worker for an urgent meeting. Hannah is able to explain that when she met her friend David at the cafeteria where she worked, they became good friends and then started to 'go out together'. David and Hannah were planning to get married but were nervous about letting their families know. David lives with his mother who is dependent on him for her own support needs. This throws up many dilemmas for the family and for the social worker. Has Hannah been exposed to risk? Was she having unprotected sex? Was she being exploited by an older, non disabled man?

A key driver for personalisation was the government White Paper, *Valuing People: A New Strategy for Learning Disability for the 21st Century* (DH 2001). This paper set out 11 key objectives based on the principles of rights, choice, independence and inclusion. There is a tension here, that although learning disability campaigners spearheaded the evolution of personalisation, it is often learning disabled people themselves who are seen as the most vulnerable sector of disabled people. In Hannah's story, both her family and the social worker are concerned about her vulnerability and risks of sexual abuse. As two consenting adults Hannah and David have the right to have a sexual relationship but need clear guidance on the risks involved and how to protect themselves. It is agreed that Hannah will have regular medical checks and support with contraception.

Issues arising

Personalisation is a concept which is shaping the way that professionals, services and service users see the future for supporting adults. The case study challenges traditional ideas of professionalism and explores where the practitioner needs to provide help and advice and when they may need to withdraw. The Coalition for Independent Living (2011) which provides a national peer brokerage service, has developed the notion of 'a continuum of professional behaviour'. This model provides a sliding scale of support which ranges from under-involvement at one end to over-involvement at the other end of the continuum. The middle zone is referred to as 'the zone of helpfulness'. Pitching the level of professional support to offer the right level of intervention requires the social work skills of deep interpersonal communication, emotional intelligence and sensitivity. Hugman (1998a) refers to the changes in professionalism as 'a return to professionalism based on principles of empowerment rather than elitism. This is consistent with an emphasis on ensuring that the work we put in to helping people resolves their difficulties and that the support is well targeted' (Hugman 1998b).

Question to consider

What balance between risks and choices do you think need to be considered for Hannah?

You may have decided that there are risks to be addressed from the social worker, the family and the individual's perspectives. The assessment of risks may differ in terms of how they are identified and prioritised, but the important factor is that there has been an open dialogue where the service user is in the centre and has the opportunity to think through the issues with the right level of help. Hannah may need support to recognise the potential dangers of certain actions and how to manage risk safely and still enjoy individual choices and independence.

Valuing People Now (DH 2009) recognises the importance of the community as the central plank of the reform agenda for achieving better and more integrated housing for learning disabled adults. Part of this initiative is to involve service users and carers in the planning and redesign of services and community housing. There still remains confusion about whether people with learning disabilities have the capacity to sign a tenancy agreement and live in their own home. *Valuing People Now* has developed a guide (Pannell and Harker 2010) to help families, carers and professionals to encourage and support someone who is entering a contract as a tenant or home owner and offers ongoing advice and support about home management and finance (2011).

CASE STUDY 5.4

Alain is 74 years old and lives in London although he was born in Tunisia and moved to the UK with his family as a young boy. Until very recently Alain has been a long term carer for his wife, who died of cancer. Alain now lives alone in his own home, although he has a supportive network of friends and relatives who live nearby. Following the death of his wife Alain experienced depression and became very withdrawn and isolated. His physical health became a concern due to diabetes and angina. At a multi-professional review held at the local hospital the hospital based social worker arranged a follow up home visit to re-assess Alain due to his changing circumstances.

Following the assessment process and application for funding it was agreed that Alain would be offered a direct payment. This is a sum of money which is paid directly to the individual for them to arrange their own support. Alain was able to supplement his direct payment with benefit entitlements and his own personal pension. Alain was very clear about how he wanted to use his personal budget; to have an annual holiday in Tunisia and to return to his previous love of photographic art. Alain planned to advertise for his own personal assistant to support him at home with practical tasks such as shopping, cleaning, cooking, etc. to free him up to return to his art. Alain's community nurse and GP raised concerns about Alain's frail health and risks of him becoming vulnerable at home on his own and travelling abroad independently. These concerns were raised with the social worker who arranged a joint home visit with Alain to talk through the concerns.

Issues arising

The involvement of health and social care practitioners working together as part of a person's support plan can create differences in perspectives based on the values and ethics integral to each profession. The medical model is the primary focus for professionals working within a health setting. Practitioners with a nursing qualification may tend to perceive the person as 'needy' and requiring professional support to manage the problem or individual impairment which has a medical or biological diagnosis. Swain and French (2008) view this as akin to the 'personal tragedy' theory, where illness and disability is seen as a personal burden and a tragedy. In contrast, the social model, which is implicit within social work core values, would emphasise the rights of the individual as a citizen to make independent choices and would perceive society as creating the barriers that can cause people who are ill, disabled or elderly to feel excluded from opportunities available to others. It is important to state, however, that the division of the medical and social models is by no means clear cut between different professions and nursing training will also include the importance of the individual as part of society and the importance of recovery and rehabilitation. With reference to the situation for Alain, the tensions arising from the staff from different professional disciplines may be linked to the central theories which inform practice for nursing and social work staff being different in their emphasis although not mutually exclusive.

Linked research

The case study mirrors a steady increase in the number of older people who are experiencing self directed support in England. A report by 'Skills for Care 'State of Adult Social Care Workforce (Eborall et al. 2010) 'captures data about the 'demographic time bomb of a rapidly aging population with an ever greater incidence of age-related and long term conditions'. The report has researched that the number of older people who were receiving direct payments in 2010 was 114 500, many of whom will also be employing their own personal carers. The report also estimates that by 2041 the number of people in England aged 85 or more will rise from almost 1 million in 2005 to around 3.2 million. Estimated predictions see an increase in personal assistant posts to 1.2 million and a reduction in demand for residential nursing support. The report also considers the change to the work role for support staff and social workers, moving towards less frequent and more stringent assessments and reviews and more community based advice and guidance and reduced day and domiciliary support.

Question to consider

Thinking about the significant changes that Alain wants to make in his life, would you consider there to be both advantages and disadvantages to reflect on in both the medical and social perspectives?

You may have identified the emphasis on biological health issues by the medical staff involved in Alain's care. This puts a focus on the health impairments as a determining factor to restricting his choices. The social model would emphasise the strengths and how barriers can be lifted to enable Alain to reflect his individuality and aspirations. It is however important to recognise the reality of health impairments and ensure that these are not ignored in favour of achieving plans which may put the individual in danger and where risks have not been carefully considered. The delicate balance of promoting personal rights and aspirations yet also ensuring that risk is managed and responsibility is taken to ensure that individuals who may be vulnerable are protected is now considered in more detail.

Service user's rights and responsibilities

We have considered the impact of personalisation for a range of individuals and their carers, and also thought about the implications for practitioners. We will now look at the shifting power balance that has been created by personalisation, giving increased responsibility to individuals in their new role as employers of their own personal assistants. A service user may now have control of the resources a local authority has allocated to meet their needs. For many the decision will be taken to use the allocated budget to employ their own personal assistant. The mechanics of setting up the stages to assess, cost and monitor the personal plan has been the central concern of practitioners and planners, with less emphasis placed on the working relationship between the individual and their paid carer (Leece and Peace 2010: 2)

Leece explores the notions of independence and autonomy in the report 'Developing new understandings of independence and autonomy in the personalised relationship' (Leece and Peace 2010). There is an interesting tension between having the independence to employ a support worker yet being dependent on that person to carry out often personal and essential tasks which can create an interdependent relationship. The notion of 'decisional autonomy' refers to the ability to take responsibility for what needs to be done, yet requiring the help to make this happen. One of the direct payment users in Leece's study summed up her intention to remain as independent as possible while recognising the need for help to achieve this: 'Different people have got different views of independence. Me, I see independence as being in control of your life. It doesn't mean particularly not being able to dress yourself or toilet yourself or anything like that' (Direct Payment User).

Much of the research and indeed the success of self directed support has been focused on those adults with the capacity to be able to demonstrate what support they need and how this will be delivered. Certainly there has been less emphasis on those people with complex needs who may lack capacity in some areas of their lives to be able to control what support is provided. It may be useful here to offer a definition of what 'complex needs' actually means. The term has been used to describe people with learning disabilities who have significant additional needs: 'the term "complex needs" is used to describe a range of multiple and additional needs that people with learning disabilities may have. This can include people with profound and multiple learning disabilities and people whose behaviour presents a challenge' (DH 2009: 38).

Reflective exercise 5.3

Pause to reflect on the reasons why people with more complex support needs have been under-represented in the numbers of service users who have accessed personal funding and support.

Much of the material covered in this chapter so far and within the text as a whole has touched on the ideology of disability that permeates society and the debates around protection from harm and abuse which have often hampered the movement of disabled people to achieve more control over their lives. The interdependency of individuals with multiple and severe disabilities with their family and relatives and the high costs of supporting a person with complex needs are all contributing factors. Perhaps your ideas can be summed up in these key points:

- There exists a culture of low expectations of people with this high level of need, contributing to the 'fear of change' by the person, their family and professionals.
- The focus on resource allocation by local authorities can overshadow and restrict the scope for personal support planning, particularly where needs are very high.
- The transition from block contracted and building based provision to individual support has been much slower for people with complex needs. Many local authorities have taken the decision to retain their traditional residential and day services for those with very high support needs.
- Specialist support services such as advocacy and 'Best Interest Assessors' are under resourced and have not been able to keep up with the rising demand.
- Self assessment for people with high needs requires very intensive support from social workers.
- There exists a fear of risk-taking for people who are vulnerable due to their complex needs.
- Partnership working between health and social care is an important factor for ensuring that funding streams are integrated and that plans are transparent and integrated. This has posed some challenges in practical implementation of support plans for people with learning, physical and health needs.

The many obstacles facing individuals and families who want to make the transition from traditional group care support to direct payments are slowly being faced and eradicated although the sector of people with complex needs remains under-represented within social care services. As stated by Denise Platt, Chair of the CSCI, 'If we get it right for people with complex needs, it is likely that we'll get it right for everyone.'

The following snapshot of a young man with severe learning disabilities and a range of behaviours described as challenging shows how changes can be brought about as the move to independent living is achieved. The outcome is explained by the parent:

> My son David now lives in his own home in the same village as me, supported by a team of staff. He was previously excluded from a specialist out-of-area service as he was 'too challenging'. With the right support in the right environment he now enjoys a good quality of life with a range of social networks within his local community. But I had to make this happen – otherwise he would have been 'put into' a residential care home which would not have met his needs and not been close to his family. But his housing is at risk because of the government housing changes – and I will have to fight to keep it. (Tizard Learning Disability Review, Volume 16, issue 2, April 2011);

We have touched on this very complex relationship between risk, rights and respon-sibilities and illustrated this by considering experiences of individuals with a spectrum of different support needs. In addition to people with complex needs being under-represented in those experiencing self directed support there are other minority groups such as black and ethnic service users. A study by Stuart (2006) focused on the direct experiences of black and minority ethnic individuals in relation to the process of accessing personal support. The study identifies linguistic, cultural and religious barriers which created challenges in accessing the support, information and advocacy they required to process through the stages of gaining a personal budget and also in employing a personal assistant from a similar ethnic cultural background.

Chapter summary

Personalisation needs to be kept simple to be able to embrace the diverse and chal-lenging requirements of all adults needing social care and health care support. The In Control original seven step model introduced at the beginning of the chapter needs to be kept as straightforward and transparent as possible to avoid bureaucracy creeping in and restrictions being imposed. Andrew Tyson (2011) promotes the need to 'strip back' personalisation and to trust the people who use adult services to know best about the kind of support they require: 'different approaches are used for people with different impairments and in different circumstances' (Tyson 2011).

Personalisation is moving ahead, despite the resource limitations and the many challenges we have touched on throughout the chapter. The Coalition Government plan to extend the current 30 per cent target for councils in England to roll out personal budgets to a much higher percentage and to link this with the NHS reforms by offering personal budgets across both social care and health.

An article in the *Guardian* by David Brindle, 'Are direct payments still living up to their name?', (Brindle, 2011) explores an independent evaluation carried out with In Control, 'Think Local, Act Personal', which reported that between half and three quarters of budget holders felt that there had been a positive impact on most aspects of their daily lives. Carers were slightly less positive with 60 per cent feeling that the general quality of their life had been improved. This information needs to be balanced however, with other information gained by the research, which identified that many of the budgets counted as direct payments are actually 'managed' or 'virtual' personal budgets where a sum of money has not been directly allocated to an individual service user or carer. This is a useful point to consider, as flexibility is necessary in the delivery of personal budgets, particularly for people with higher support needs such as older, frailer people who may not want the responsibility of 'managing the money' directly.

In considering how personalisation can progress, it is worth focusing on very recent developments on co-production and utilising the expertise and wisdom of service users themselves. This builds upon Leadbeater's publications on developing self directed support: 'Many of the ingredients – direct payments, person-centred planning, peer and family support teams and user led organisations – are well established approaches for people with learning and physical disabilities' (Leadbeater et al. 2008: 255). Co-production has emerged to provide a general description of the process whereby service users work alongside professionals as partners in the delivery of services. This may be the future path for personalisation and longer term survival in the current social, financial and political climate. The use of peer support networks may be the best way forward in transferring knowledge and capabilities and reducing the distinction between users and recipients and providers and consumers of services. The sense of reciprocity and mutuality offered by the values implicit within personalisation should enable service users to be both providers and recipients.

This chapter has considered the many dilemmas, questions and uncertainties that are part and parcel of personalisation. The main thrust of the chapter has been to promote the personal experiences of service users and carers of self directed support, through case studies. The last word will go to a quote from a young man who made the transition from a group day care setting to having a direct payment: 'Now I take great care of myself. My self esteem and confidence are growing day by day. People say to me, "How do you feel now?" I say, "I've got my life back again"'. (Webster 2008).

References

Beresford, P. (2007) *The Changing Roles and Tasks of Social Work from Service Users' Perspectives: Shaping Our Lives.* London: General Social Care Council.

Brindle, D. (2011) Are Direct Payments still living up to their name? *Guardian*, 22 June.

Buckner, I. and Yeandle, S. (2011) *Valuing Carers 2001. Calculating the Value of Carer's Support.* London: University of Leeds and Care U.K.

Coalition for Independent Living (CIL) (2011) www.brokerage@c-i-l.org.uk

DH (Department of Health) (2001) *Valuing People: A New Strategy for Learning Disability for the 21st Century.* London: Department of Health.

DH (2007) *Putting People First: A Shared Vision and Commitment to the Transformation of Adult Social Care.* London: DH.

DH (2009) *Valuing People Now.* London: HMSO.

Duffy, S. (2010) The citizenship theory of social justice: exploring the meaning of personalisation for social workers. *Journal of Social Work Practice*, 24(3) September 2010: 253–67.

Eborall, C., Fenton, W. and Woodrow, S. (2010) *The State of the Adult Social Care Work force in England*. 2010 Executive Summary, Skills for Care. www.skillsforcare.org.uk (pdf 2.32b).

Flynn, M. (2006) 'Developing the role of personal assistants. Researched and compiled for a Skills for Care pilot project examining new and emerging roles in social care.' University of Sheffield. 28th March LSE.

Hugman, R. (1998a) But is it social work? Some reflections on mistaken identities. *British Journal of Social Work*, 39(6): 1138–53.

Hugman, R. (1998b) *Social Welfare and Social Value*. sciencesarts.unsw.edu.au/staff/Richard-hugman-12 2hlml.

IBSEN (2008) 'The National Evaluation of the Individual Budgets pilot programme.' Dept. Health Social Policy Research Unit York University.

In Control (2007) '*Making a Support Plan*'. London: In Control.

Kirkpatrick, K. (2011) A home of my own: progress on enabling people with learning disabilities to have choice and control over where and with whom they live. *Tizard Learning Disability Review*, 16(2): 7–13.

Leadbeater, C. (2004) *Personalisation through Participation: A New Script for Public Services*. London: Demos.

Leadbeater C., Bartlett, J. and Gallagher, N. et al. (2008) *Making it Personal* London: Demos.

Leece, J. and Peace, S. (2010) Developing new understandings of independence and autonomy in the personalised relationship. *British Journal of Social Work*, 40(6): 1847–65.

Lefevre, M. (2005) Facilitating practice, learning and assessment: the influence of relationships in social work education. *Social Work Education*, 24(5) 1–19.

Moran, N., Arksey, H., Glendinning, C. et al. (2011) Personalisation and carers: whose rights? whose benefits? *British Journal of Social Work* 1–19.

Pannell, J. and Harker, M. (2010) *Finding a Place to Live: Help with your Plans*. Housing Options Resource Park. Valuing People Now publications. www.housingoption.org.uk (mita.shah@dh.gsi.gov.uk).

Social Work Reform Board. www.communitycare.co.uk/socialworkreformboard.

Sowerby, D. (2010) What sort of helping relationships are needed to make Personalisation happen and how can organisations be developed to support this? *Journal of Social Work Practice*, 24(3): 269–82.

Stuart, D. (2006) *Will Community-based Support Services Make Direct Payments a Viable Option for Black and Minority Ethnic Service Users and Carers?* Stakeholder Participation Race Equality Discussion Paper 1. Social Care Institute for Excellence. www.scie.org.uk.

Swain, J. and French, S. (2008) *Disability on Equal Terms*. London: Sage.

Tyson, A. (2011) *Personalisation and Learning Disabilities: A Handbook*. Hove: OLM Pavilion.

Webster, K. (2008) From a Service to a Life; A Yes Man No More. *Learning Disability Today*, 34.

6

Dreams to reality: the way forward

Introduction

The roll out of personalisation is still in its fledgling stage, and studies into how best to implement the agenda while surmounting the challenges it brings will no doubt continue long into the future. But for the people who are experiencing personalisation at a grass roots level, one thing is certain: change. For individual service users, carers, self-funders, social workers, commissioners, service providers, health care professionals and many more on the health and social care spectrum, changes to systems, roles, responsibilities and everyday life are inevitable. This chapter aims to address those changes and consider how best to manage them for the benefit of all parties, while looking forward to consider new ways of working that will continue to drive change in the right direction.

Personalisation by its very nature presents an opportunity to work alongside service users to find new ways of operating and managing the change process. By doing so, when personalisation is implemented it will make sense to service users and those working in adult social care. Social workers and allied health professionals can offer support and skills to develop and shape these emerging ways of working, and generate new ideas based on the principles of co-design and co-production.

How do we measure the changes that personalisation brings to people?

It is important that when we look at research into the changes that personalisation will bring to people, we constructively critique the methodologies used to obtain results. We must consider the nature of measuring change, and assess the factors that we consider to be indicators of success. Much of the research and evaluations of personalisation programmes have, up to now, tended to focus on the experience of budget holding or a direct payment as an indicator of the success of personalisation. This was certainly the case in the IBSEN and Demos reports (see below). Little focus has been given to the overall experience of personalised services, the process of self-directed support, support planning, person centred planning or peer support. This emphasis on budget holding means that the importance of *supporting* people in a personalised way is pushed to the sidelines.

This view has filtered into local government approaches to measuring the success rate of the personalisation agenda. Local authorities and service providers tend to view the number of allocated budgets as an indicator of success, rather than looking at aspects such as quality of life outcomes. The merging of budget holding and personalisation is troubling as there is a risk of diluting personalisation to a mere pursuit for endless choice and consumption.

The impact of this for service users is that the meaning of personalisation and the changes it can bring are not properly communicated. The original vision for person-alisation stressed that factors such as active citizenship, service quality and profes-sional and social support methods are vital for the success of the project. We are not devoting enough time to asking people how and if their lives have been transformed by personalisation and instead focus on the differences that budget holding has had. To measure change successfully we must distinguish between the delivery mode (the budget) and the approach (person centred support or self directed support). However, measuring the qualitative changes that personalisation brings for individual people, and scaling those findings quantitatively for research purposes, is by no means an easy task. Change in this context is highly subjective and involves working with people on a one-on-one basis to understand what transformation they wish to bring about in their lives. Unsurprisingly, to date there has been no tool developed to quantitatively and qualitatively measure the changes that personalisation brings outside of budget holding.

However, researchers have tried to measure this sort of change by using existing tools. Some have used the ASCOT tool, a questionnaire developed by Kent University that asks the service user how they would rate various aspects of their current social care situation on a numeric scale. Relative satisfaction scores are then calculated after the questionnaire is repeated after social care services have been put in place. Similarly In Controls POET (Personal Budgets Outcomes Evaluation Tool) uses well-being indicators to evaluate the impact of personal budgets. Techniques such as this are arguably not specific enough to the intricacies of an individual's situation. Asking people to rate fixed aspects of their social care situation on a scale is problematic – it presupposes the things that people are or are not satisfied with are directly linked to budget holding as opposed to other factors in their lives on which budget holding does not impact. We need to endeavour to create more tools that would allow us to carry out such research to measure the overall impact of personalisation, in a way that would benefit individuals and provide a data set for use in local and national quantita-tive evaluations of the success of personalisation beyond mere budget allocation. We could be measuring success and satisfaction in meeting outcomes set in the action plan of a support plan – every action plan is different in content, but the yearly review of success or failure in meeting goals is universal. If this data were anonymised and collated, it could be analysed.

The POET survey also showed that local authorities aren't all doing self directed support in the same way – many have added and subtracted different levels of bureaucracy. It would appear that the old system – care management, and the policies and procedures around it – get in the way of personalisation (see Centre for Welfare reform 2011). This method of analysis would require all people to have an action plan from a good, well constructed self directed support plan.

More effort needs to be put into developing measures that wholeheartedly subscribe to person-centred outcomes as defined by the individual and which are geared to fill gaps in provision that would allow individuals to live the life they wish. These tools need to be developed by and with individuals who experience the system rather than the organisations that provide services within or outside of statutory services by working in co-production.

What research has been done and how effective has it been in measuring the changes?

Bearing in mind the aforementioned issues with current research approaches, what can we glean from existing data about the changes that personalisation is bringing to individuals?

There are three key pieces of research and evaluation on the changes that personalisation have made to people's lives: the IBSEN report (Glendinning et al. 2008) carried out by the University of York's Social Policy research unit; a 2008 report from policy think-tank Demos (Leadbeater et al. 2008); and a study by the University of Lancaster and In Control from 2011 (Hatton and Waters 2011). They all looked at budget giving and how satisfied or dissatisfied people were with how the budget affected their satisfaction with certain aspects of their lives, from satisfaction with care to civic engagement.

The general findings from the IBSEN report were that people who took individual budgets were more satisfied with their care than those who did not (49 per cent compared with 43 per cent). Their research also found no great difference in quality of life scores between the control group and the individual budget holders group (Glendinning et al. 2008). The Demos report found a positive result for people who took personal budgets based on civic engagement. Demos highlighted one evaluation that showed 63 per cent of respondents stating that they take more part in community life after the implementation of personal budgets while 2 per cent of people stated the contrary (Leadbeater et al. 2008). The national personal budgets survey carried out by University of Lancaster and In Control analysed data from 1,114 personal budget users across 10 local authorities and found that on most roughly 70 per cent of respondents reported improved quality of life, while only 3–8 per cent stated that their quality of life had deteriorated (Hatton and Waters 2011). In contrast, the same study showed that very few people felt their personal budget had led to greater community engagement, such as personal budgets making no difference to people in the following areas: getting and keeping a paid job (88 per cent), people volunteering and helping their local community (77 per cent), people choosing where they live and who they live with (60 per cent), and people's relationships with friends (52 per cent) (Hatton and Waters 2011). In the main the focus of all three reports remains on budget giving and budget holding. The quantitative analysis is not significant enough to draw conclusive results about the overall impact of personalisation in bringing about positive changes in individuals' lives. Also what is not clear from the research is the overall amount of support that individuals had when taking up a personal budget. There may be reasons outside of taking a personal budget that effects the individual's ability to exercise choice and control. More in-depth research is needed to examine this further. However, if the most recent findings from In Control indicate that personal budgets are failing to make a significant difference in as key an aspect as civic and community participation, what additional factors might be needed to improve that situation?

Support is vital

If we were to take the experience of self-funders as a litmus test for whether holding a budget leads to active citizenship we would recognise that personalisation is about more than simply giving people money and choice. We frequently find that self-funders are more likely to experience disadvantage and exploitation in the open market place without appropriate support to spend their resources. As was pointed out in the Putting People First analysis of self-funders in the social care market: 'Time and again, people described the struggle to obtain information, advice or advocacy to help them in making life-changing decisions' (SCIE 2011). The most frequent experience cited in that report was of people being given a list of care homes and left to find their own way.

Having sufficient resources to self fund is not, of itself, any guarantee that people will have greater control over their situation, or be equipped to be able to make the best decisions for their situation (SCIE 2011). The need for people to have financial information and advice has been identified as a critical gap. This is of particular concern 'because of the evidence that significant numbers of people make both poor care and financial decisions without access to this information and advice' (SCIE 2011). Local authorities had a target to provide locally provided information, advice and guidance services that are universally available, however this has not yet happened across the board. The lack of information highlights that those who have less social support are likely to gain the least from personalisation because information remains patchy.

Given the experience of self-funders (who are effectively their own budget holders), if personalisation is reduced merely to budget holding, it may put people in danger of becoming overwhelmed by choice, lacking control and not being advised and directed towards appropriate support. Research commissioned by CSIP has explored the experiences of older people and those with mental health problems in more detail and shown that personal budgets and the processes underpinning them can work for these groups if they have the right kind of help and support. This help and support took the form of service users 'receiving help and support writing their support plans with the help of family, friends and social workers' (Leadbeater et al. 2008: 33). According to Leadbeater et al. 'Investing in well-trained people to support budget-holders to develop their support plan will be critical to make self-directed services a success' (p. 51).

The need for help and support was further reinforced by a report published by the Office for Disability Issues (ODI) which looked at what kinds of support might be needed to help individuals make the best out of personalisation. The findings of the ODI report highlighted the importance of support from peers in user-led organisations, or networks of disabled people. This was felt to be a 'vital part of the system and critical to the successful delivery of personalised services' (ODI 2011: 93). In addition it was noted that help and support for self-funders should take the following into account:

- Social workers need to be aware of their duty to assess everyone regardless of their financial circumstances, and not just those whose care will be paid by the local authority.

- Social workers should challenge attempts by managers to 'screen out' self-funders from advice and support.

- Social workers should direct self-funders to appropriate sources of advice and support.

(SCIE 2011)

This lack of available information, advice and guidance and support, presents an opportunity for organisations working with individuals to develop innovative ways to communicate with service users, harnessing the power of technology and tools used by both the media and design industry to convey complicated concepts into a simple messages.

CASE STUDY 6.1

MySupportBroker.com

mysupportbroker.com is an online web service that has successfully brought together both social workers and individual disabled and older people (known as 'peers') to provide support brokerage in the community. What is particularly interesting about this organisation is the use of multi media to enable individuals to tell their stories of support planning and to break down difficult concepts such as personalisation into digestible videos. They have recently produced a privacy policy for their website that has been put together in collaboration with internet privacy experts, individuals and social workers. Increasingly organisations will need to find innovative ways to share and pool their assets thereby breaking down the old top down hierarchies by providing services together.

Choice and control: citizenship or consumerism?

It is a widely supported idea that personalisation will change and increase the level of choice and control to which service users have access. However, the factors determining someone's ability to choose have been given less attention. The normative assumptions about choice are beginning to be challenged. Recent academics have argued that policies promoting choice 'favour people with existing financial and social capital', and that these resources are unequally distributed (Clarke et al. quoted in Stevens et al. 2011: 262). A critical debate has emerged which questions whether personalisation encourages a consumerist role for those who receive support, or if personalisation supports a role for the service user based on citizenship and social inclusion (Duffy 2010).

The consumerist model sees a role for local authorities in developing the market and asks providers to set up the right kind of goods and services and business for budget holder to buy from. The citizenship model on the other hand reserves a strong role for the state and providers in regulating provision and developing and fostering links and support networks between people, so that they can participate in day to day activities to a greater extent.

The consumerist model turns people into passive recipients of goods and services – they become clients, or customers, who through holding a personal budget are able to exercise choice within an open market. However, this presumes a positive view of the market and makes assumptions about how the open market functions: a) that consumers are provided with accurate information; b) that competition and supply and demand are healthy; and c) that customers always have choice and power.

Those who have argued against the consumerist model espouse the belief that a state funded social care system will bring about change for people because they believe that the state is more likely to encourage people's inclusion into society as active citizens. Simon Duffy's 'Citizenship model' outlines this distinction (Duffy 2010). A citizenship model of personalisation recognizes the limits of solely shifting buying power to people who receive support. As has been highlighted above, the act of budget holding is not enough and support is required. Supporters of social justice models see that there is a need for statutory bodies and providers to develop social networks, encourage mutual support and co-production, and actively support people to play a role within their community. The normative presumption here is that state solutions are always the best and that the state is capable of innovation to support change for individuals. However, change is not something that you can do *for* people, it is something that you do *with* people. This act of working in partnership or co-production is more likely to support transformative change. Research has indicated that 'co-production, where it has been happening successfully, has generally been outside nationally funded services that are supposed to achieve this, and usually despite – rather than because of – administrative systems inside public services' (Boyle et al. 2006: 10).

As has been mentioned above, the missing ingredient is support to help make informed choices. Without support in place, researchers argue that choices in and of themselves can be difficult and paralysing. Professor Renata argues that 'psychologists have seen that overwhelming choice creates the feeling of anxiety in regard to what I really want, but it also in some way pacifies people; people are quite often frozen in a state of indecisiveness when there are too many choices' (Renata, 2010). She argues that having increased choice does not help to create social change on the level of individuals and that it can have the opposite effect of deluding individuals into thinking that they have control when in fact they don't.

Furthermore, according to Barnes and Prior (1995) focusing on choice brings limited benefits and can disempower people whereas user empowerment is more likely to be achieved through utilising the experiences and opinions of users, giving them a collective say in policy making.

What is important to consider is not just the volume of choice we give or present to individuals but how much we support them to be able to make informed choices and to become empowered through the process of personalisation. This will mean working at a pace that is acceptable to an individual, and understanding that empowerment will mean different things to different people. We should understand what level of support a person needs, and offer support that allows them to make informed choices with as much or as little control as they would like to have. Plus we must ensure that those who cannot or do not want to take control have access to adequate person centered services to help them live the life they want to live.

CASE STUDY 6.2

C-I-L: Peer Support

James had been on a direct payment for over five years. However, he did not have any form of support to manage this fund and the budget had been given to a local direct payments support service to manage. James was not offered any avenue to learn how to manage these funds. He consequently felt trapped with little choice and control. This was exacerbated by his care workers being paid by the direct payments service and therefore he felt that his staff were not accountable to him. James joined a personal budgets pilot in 2009. He chose to work with another disabled person throughout the process who became his peer broker. Together they wrote James a support plan. His goal was to manage his own funds and to go abroad and travel independently. Together with his peer broker they established James Ltd and they now manage the personal budget together. James has learned from Frances (his peer broker) how to use Internet banking and how much all the care workers get paid. He has designed a set of house rules and does all of the supervision of the staff with Frances. As a direct impact of working with James, Frances was also able to get paid employment, which she did not have prior to working with James. Frances is now an independent peer broker and works with a number of disabled and older people. James also gets travel training and frequently uses the bus by himself and has been to Spain on holiday.

The case study demonstrates that where there is the opportunity for individuals to be supported to take an active role they feel liberated to choose a range of ways to spend their personal budgets which goes outside of the traditional purchasing of care. However, these choices are in essence mainstream activities that many other people take for granted. What is interesting about this case study is that it highlights that people with social care needs want to access the community. The other interesting point to highlight is that these services already exist in the marketplace and there is nothing out of the ordinary or particularly specialist in the things that James wanted to do. What this small example indicates is that disabled and older people could have a significant role in supporting the wider economy.

What is less clear from the example is how specialist and niche services will be paid for: for example, activities such as advocacy and specialist services for people with particular conditions. Most importantly, how will these sorts of services be funded when it is no longer cost effective for service providers to run them?

A more detailed analysis of budget spend across personal budget holders is needed to be able to draw any valid conclusions about these trends.

The changing role of the social worker

In recent times social workers have complained they feel disconnected from their 'therapeutic' role and unable to deliver on the person centred values and goals that initially drew them to the profession (Leadbeater et al. 2008). The care management role forces workers to be risk managers, gatekeepers and controllers. Their scope for exercising judgement and discretion has been limited by rules and lack of resources. If the goal of personalisation is to go beyond budget giving and budget holding, there is a need to change the daily business processes of front line workers. The relationship that is conceptualised by supporters of self directed support, such as Simon Duffy, rests on involvement, power sharing, accountability and shared decision making. They state that a fundamental shift along the entire care support process, from assessment through to evaluation, is required.

We do not know what the long term changes to both resources and infrastructure will bring. All current evaluations of personalisation have been conducted with existing social care systems and resources in place. Essentially what has been evaluated is mapping new models of social care on top of existing provision.

Recent research from the Joseph Roundtree Foundation's 'Standards We Expect' project highlighted the fact that development of person centred support is inhibited by a continuing culture of social care that works against the philosophies and values of person centred support. (JRF 2011). However, as personal budgets become the norm across all of social care the social work shift – since 1993 – to care management might well be reversed.

CASE STUDY 6.3

'A New Script for Social Work'

Yorkshire and Humber Joint Improvement Partnership have argued that for personalisation to become a reality, a 'New Script for Social Work' is needed.

The 'new script' argues that much of what social workers need to do:

- cannot be done for people, it must be done with them;
- cannot be done without support: personalisation must be delivered by working in partnership with citizens.

According to the Yorkshire and Humber Joint Improvement Partnership,

> a big problem for social workers is that the old system gets in the way; the old care management system makes it hard to do social work. It's really hard to empower people without entitlements, to strengthen capacity focussing only on needs, to connect to the community from inside segregated services, to build safe networks without family, friends or love.

(Centre for Welfare Reform 2011)

They state that currently, in care management, 'systems sit on systems like sedimentary rock' and that personalisation cannot be seen as yet another system on top of the existing care management process. The entire system should be transformed to deliver Self Directed Support, according to the model illustrated in this flow chart:

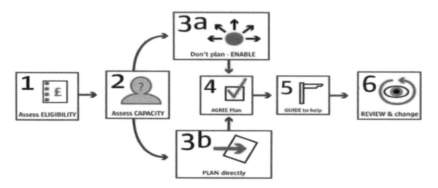

(Reproduced with permission from the Centre for Welfare Reform http://www.centreforwelfarereform.org/)

They believe that this system will mean that social workers can empower people, tell people their budget, strengthen capacity, focus on personal outcomes, access community, use funding flexibly, build safe networks and work with family, friends and others.

Working on equal terms

An emerging theme in the literature on personalisation suggests that professionals might play a more facilitative role in assisting individuals to identify their own support needs and commission support that works for them. Working 'with' people rather than doing things 'to' or 'for' people is central to making personalisation meaningful to individuals. We need to shift the relationship towards co-producing services and solutions with individuals where both parties are working alongside each other to support the best possible outcomes. However, as has been stated above it not easy for professionals to play a facilitative role within the current care management mode. A study in an unnamed London borough showed that some professionals had reservations about the organisation of the new system of personalisation; however, most social workers were positive about the results. They expressed that assisting people to be independent reflected the ideal of social work that attracted them to the job in the first place (Williams and Tyson 2010).

To allow self directed support to become the process by which social workers operate we must also change the way we think about risk. Recommendations from SCIE's report on risk in personalisation (SCIE 2011) include promoting risk enablement approaches which are person focused, ensuring people have informed choice, and adapting organisational systems to support a culture of risk taking (Carr 2010a).

The changing role of the Commissioner

Exactly how the social care market will develop is unclear. 'Early indications suggest change will be gradual rather than revolutionary. There will be less demand for residential care homes and day centres and an increase in the demand for personal assistants and informal support' (Leadbeater et al. 2008: 60). There is a risk that as large block contracts are de-commissioned, building based provision will be lost, which may have an impact on budget holders' ability to meet and socialise. The impact of these commissioning decisions is unknown (Needham 2010).

Commissioners have not yet facilitated enough market development to be able to provide optimal choice and control for budget holders (Carr 2010b). In Essex it was reported that budget holders' power as consumers was undermined because of a lack of affordable alternative (OPM 2010). The Essex pilot also showed that budget holders rely on personal or professional recommendations which had the impact of privileging those with wider social and support networks. Those without such help had to make it up as they went along (OPM (2010). This example further demonstrates the argument that support is vital.

Leaving budget holders to make guesses about their social care does not seem appropriate. On the other hand it is impossible for any market to develop or innovative solutions to emerge without individuals having access to more than their social care budget. Commissioning budgets are not yet being included in the personal budget and therefore the spending power of individuals with personal care needs remain restrictive.

To respond to the growing number of personal budget holders an increasing number of organisations have attempted to build E-market solutions such as Shop4Support, which was supported by In Control, and Quickheart supported by Stockport council. These adhere to the consumerism model rather than the social justice model, as discussed previously. This further exacerbates and confines the individual's role to that of a passive consumer. It is questionable if current social care commissioners have the necessary skills and training to assist in shaping the social care marketplace. Greater understanding and research will be needed in mapping the needs of individuals service users to assist commissioners. Again working in a co-produced way is an innovative way to build relevant community services. It is important that this co-produced way of working does not result in a quest for choice and consumption.

Changes for service providers

> Traditional service providers – public, private and voluntary – will face upheaval and change.
>
> (Leadbeater et al. 2008: 60)

Market development opportunities continue to be restricted and service providers have not yet begun to market themselves directly to service users. Choice remains medical model focused and not geared towards service users accessing wider community services. There is space for services and innovations to develop which harness the social capital of individuals as citizens to share and connect as opposed to buy and consume. When services are co-produced, the traditional perception of users as passive recipients of services is thrown out in favour of a new approach that sees them as assets to the service. This means that services can become jointly managed and produced with professionals.

The way ahead: co-production and social care

As has been discussed, successful personalisation requires social care workers to devolve power toward service users. This devolution cannot occur without working in partnership with service users to enable them to take on increasing responsibility. Building community capacity is central to that.

The coalition government has committed itself to accelerating the pace of personalisation in social care, and expanding it to other areas such as health, with the national roll out of personal health budgets. They have set a target that by 2015, 100 per cent of all eligible social care clients should have a personal budget. This is further supported by the Localism Bill 2010 and partnership agreements such as Think Local Act Personal 2010, which support the further devolution of power away from the state and directly to individuals and communities. 'This Government trusts people to take charge of their lives and we will push power downwards and outwards to the lowest possible level, including individuals, neighbourhoods, professionals and communities as well as local councils and other local institutions' (Communities and Local Government 2011). This demonstrates a swing towards service users' active involvement in development and delivery.

This shift of policy focus requires further collaboration and social capital and is, in essence, co-production. Co-production recognises and harnesses the expertise of service users in shaping their own care and encourages their involvement in improving and delivering services. It challenges the dominant role of the professional and shifts the service user from the role of a passive recipient to that of a valued participant in the process on an individual and collective level (Needham 2009).

Co-production in adult care services

Research suggests that there are three different types of co-production in adult social care services:

1   **Compliance (descriptive)** Co-production takes place at the stage of service delivery, as carers and people who use services collaborate to achieve results. People using services make contributions at each stage of service provision but they are not involved in implementation.

    Weaknesses of the compliance level Despite the acknowledgement that care services cannot be produced without input from the people who use services, the compliance tier offers little opportunity for real change by or for the people who use services because it is about complying with an existing regime.

2   **Support (intermediate)** The intermediate level of co-production recognises values of people who come together to co-produce care services. It acknowledges

the input and value of service users, utilises existing support networks and improves channels for people to be involved in the shaping of services. It may include new or more involved roles for users in the recruitment and training of professionals and managers. Also it may see responsibilities being shared with the people who use services.

Weaknesses of the support level Users continue to be supporters rather than controllers or managers of the service. The expertise continues to be situated outside of the users themselves.

3   **Transformative** The most effective methods of co-production can transform services and create new relationships between the people who use them and staff. This transformative level of co-production takes 'a whole life focus', incorporating quality of life issues as well as simply clinical or service issues.

At its most effective, co-production can involve the transformation of services. The transformative level of co-production requires a relocation of power and control, through the development of new user-led mechanisms of planning, delivery, management and governance. It involves new structures of delivery to entrench co-production, rather than simply ad hoc opportunities for collaboration. It can be 'a form of citizenship in practice'.

(Needham 2009: 6)

Co-production cannot be done without support

For co-production to be successful a number of things need to happen. There needs to be support for the building of social capital for all groups in the community: without adequate support, co-production can sideline already marginalised groups as there are limits to the extent that some people can co-produce without support. Social exclusion, equality and diversity need to be taken into account to ensure that co-production does not target those who are in a position to be more involved but reaches out in a proactive way to those people who require support to take part. It is important that co-production is not seen as a means for statutory or government agencies to wash their hands of problems and issues for services users to deal with. Co-production as a means of achieving transformation needs to be sustained; however, this is challenged by the short term nature of projects and initiatives.

For co-production to be successful both staff and service users require access to training. Social care staff require training to share power with service users and service users need support to fill in skills gaps to be able to contribute. Being able to take positive risks is essential for both staff and service users as this is essential to the learning and creative process of co-production. This is important in breaking down some of the professional relationships and ensuring staff continuity so that relationships can be built. It has been reported that staff attitudes could be transformed through taking part in co-productive projects, such as a greater awareness of the contributions of people who use services and their carers, and greater recognition of the credibility of service users working as outreach workers – although they also acknowledged the pressures of time available to spend on the project (Needham 2009).

The transformative approach can come closest to fulfilling the demands of the 'Putting people first' adult social care personalisation agenda (DH 2008).

However research has indicated that 'co-production, where it has been happening successfully, has generally been outside nationally funded services that are supposed to achieve this, and usually despite – rather than because of – administrative systems inside public services' (Boyle et al. 2006: 10). This needs to be considered when forging partnerships with non-statutory agencies, voluntary organisations and user-led organisations. According to Small (2000), the transition of an individual from passive recipient of services to active subject engaging with services is at the centre of user empowerment.

Co-production is not a new delivery mechanism for social care services. It is an approach which affirms and supports an active and productive role for people who use services, and the value of collaborative relationships in delivering the outcomes negotiated with the person using the service. The development of service user involvement in the voluntary and statutory sectors has largely stemmed from user movements advocating for rights of their members like the disability movement (Beresford 2005; see Rummery and Glendinning 2000 and Ellis 2005 for examples). The aim is to develop a model where the consciousness of users and the wider community is raised and as a result the people involved are empowered to make decisions not only about the services they receive, but also in their lives as a whole. There is a hope that this in turn will be effective in bringing about change in policy and practice through allowing the voices of those receiving the services to be heard (Campbell and Oliver 1996). Barnes and Walker (1996) identified eight principles of empowerment through service user involvement and co-production:

1   It should enable personal development as well as increasing influence over services.

2   It should increase people's abilities to take control of their lives as a whole not just increase influence over services.

3   The empowerment of one person should not result in the exploitation of others, either family members or paid carers.

4   It should not be viewed as a zero sum: a partnership model should provide benefits for both partners.

5   It must be reinforced at all levels within service systems.

6   Empowerment of those who use services does not remove responsibility from those who provide them.

7   It is not an alternative to adequate resources for services.

8   It should be a collective as well as an individual process; without this people will become increasingly assertive in competing with each other.

These eight principles provide professionals with a simple check list against which they can evaluate their relationships with service users whether on a one to one basis or at an organisational level.

Case studies: co-production in action

Peer networks provide a valuable forum for independent discussion and debate away from professionals and services. One example of how co-production can enable greater choice is shown in the case study of Westminster Action Network on Disability.

CASE STUDY 6.4

Co-production easy as baking a cake

In Westminster, the project started off with an IT emphasis, initially experiencing some difficulties finding the right partners. The Council then involved the local organisation run by disabled people in Westminster, Westminster Action Network on Disability (WAND). WAND is a local disabled people's organisation, developed as a grass roots organisation whose main activities focussed on providing information and advocacy as well as promoting user engagement.

'The CAF board meetings were about people telling you what was happening it was very complicated to understand as much of it was about council and primary care trust technologies and technology companies updating about what version they were on etc.' (WAND).

'However, we then set up a business sub group with a focus on personalisation which had fewer people on it and this was much better. I felt more confidence about saying what I feel; also people were more prepared to listen to me at this meeting. Most if not all of our recommendations were given the green light. I think if I had known this I would have pushed for more changes' (WAND).

While many other local disabled peoples organisations have moved into service delivery either through choice or by necessity WAND felt strongly that this might lessen their main role of representing people.

WAND worked with the council and another organisation to develop a web-based information solution. This was developed to link brokers with service providers and potentially a wider network of support and services.

'In Westminster this will be achieved by the development of a range of integrated self-directed support software tools designed to put citizens at the centre of controlling their health and social care assessments and support plans'

On working in a co-produced way outlined above Westminster Council reflected 'We wish we'd done it sooner!'

(Equal Citizen 2011)

CASE STUDY 6.5

Up2Us

Up2us was designed by the Housing Action Charity (HACT) in response to the personalisation agenda. Up2us brings people together so they can meet others and pool their personal budget resources. Though they do not all involve a relationship of co-production between people and professionals, they are developing collective and collaborative models of support that enable people to pool their financial, personal and social resources, and to support each other and share their experience and knowledge of different support methods.

Chapter summary

Co-production is of central importance to the personalisation and transformation of adult social care services. It is relevant to all sectors in adult social care (including voluntary and independent sector providers) and for all kinds of people who use social care services (Needham 2009). Co-production 'is a positive affirmation that people can develop their own futures with the support of others including professionals' (Hunter and Ritchie 2007). What is different about co-production is that it situates individual users in the position of 'producer' of a service rather than just 'consumer' of a service or product.

If co-production is to improve outcomes in social care, it will be at the 'transformative' level, avoiding versions of co-production that simply cut costs, demand compliance or reproduce existing power relations (Needham 2009). The over reliance on budget holding and consumerism has masked the potential opportunity to develop a more collective and collaborative system of social care. Co-production offers a route away from a consumerism model. For co-production to be successful for individuals, professionals and organisations, support at every level is vital. Without community capacity building, skills sharing and peer support co-production could be reduced to an activity that is reserved for the privileged in our society.

Co-production activities alone are not sufficient to drive forward large-scale organisational culture change. However, co-productive actvities involving service users can impact significantly upon the success of any changes in relation to the services received by users rather than merely meeting the needs of the service in development and planning (Richardson 2005). To ensure that co-production pushes towards a transformative model the culture of 'me' and 'I' that currently dominates much of the practice around personalisation which promotes individualism and pushes passive recipients of care services into becoming passive consumers must be challenged. The success indicators of personalisation cannot merely be measured through the prism of budgets and increased individualism. To move beyond budgets a cultural paradigm shift is needed. Personalisation needs to move towards being about creating a culture of 'we', of 'community' and of empowerment. For this to take place a renewed belief in community and sharing is required, not just in social care, but in our society, as after all is said and done users and professional live out their lives in the community and not within social care.

Personalisation at its core should not be just about monetising peoples needs and helping them to consume but making a sizemic leap from defining people by what they buy and what their allocated budget is to valuing what they contribute instead. This involves empowering individuals to build larger roles in our society, which will bring about a stronger and healthier future for service users and professionals alike. At their best traditional social care and consumerist solutions turn people into passive recipients of the service. At their best self directed services motivate people to find and provide their own solutions to both personal and community needs.

Personalisation and the implementation of personal budgets is a theme that cuts across all government thinking. The main implication of this for users and social care professionals is that we must work together to conceptualise innovations that will support individuals to make the best out of their budgets. The other is that there is an imperative to ensure that the appropriate support exists in the community and that giving an individual a budget does not obfuscate our responsibility to protect and support community capacity so that the most vulnerable within our society are looked out for and feel safe participating in the community along with their peers and supporters.

References

Barnes, M. and Prior, D. (1995) Spoilt for choice? How consumerism can disempower public service users. *Public Money and Management*, 15: 3.

Barnes, M. and Walker, A. (1996) Consumerism versus empowerment: a principled approach to the involvement of older service users. *Policy and Politics*, 24(4): 375–93.

Beresford, P. (2005) 'Service user': regressive or liberatory terminology? *Disability & Society*, 20(4): 469–77.

Boyle, D., Clark, S. and Boyle, D. (2006) *Hidden Work: Co-production by People Outside Paid Employment*. York: Joseph Rowntree Foundation.

Campbell, J. and Oliver, M. (1996) *Disability Politics in Britain: Understanding Our Past, Changing our Future*. Routledge. London.

Carr, S. (2010a) *Enabling Risk, Ensuring Safety: Self-directed Support and Personal budgets*. Adult Services SCIE Report 36I. London: Social Care Institute for Excellence.

Carr, S. (2010b) *Personalisation, Productivity and Efficiency*. Adult Services SCIE Report 37. London: Social Care Institute for Excellence.

Centre for Welfare Reform (2011) *A New Script for Social Work*. http://www.youtube.com/watch?v=7yfkBx8OZVk (accessed 18 January 2012).

Communities and Local Government (2011) *The Localism Act*. http://www.communities.gov.uk/localgovernment/decentralisation/localismbill/ (accessed 18 January 2012).

DH (Department of Health) (2008) *Local Authority Circular LAC 1: Transforming Social Care*. London: Department of Health.

Duffy, S. (2010) The citizenship theory of social justice: exploring the meaning of personalisation for social workers. *Journal of Social Work Practice*, 24: 253–67

Ellis, K. (2005) Disability rights in practice: the relationship between human rights and social rights in contemporary social care. *Disability & Society*, 20(7): 691–704.

Equal Citizen (2011) *Co Production Easy as Baking a Cake*. http://www.dhcarenetworks.org.uk/_library/Resources/CAF/CAFProduct/Equal_Citizen_Services_-_Co-Production.pdf (accessed 22 December 2011).

Glendinning, C., Challis, D., Fernandez, J.-L. et al. (2008) *IBSEN: Evaluation of the Individual Budgets Pilot Programme, Final Report*. York: Social Policy Research Unit.

Hatton, C. and Waters, J. (2011) *Think Local, Act Personal: The National Personal Budget Survey*. London: University of Lancaster & In Control.

Hunter, S. and Ritchie, P. (2007) *Co-production and Personalisation in Social Care: Changing Relationships in the Provision of Social Care*. London: Jessica Kingsley Publishers.

Joseph Rowntree Foundation (2011) *Transforming Social Care: Sustaining Person Centred Support*.

Leadbeater, C., Bartlett, J. and Gallagher, N. (2008) *Making It Personal*. London: DEMOS.

Needham, C. (2009) *Co-production: An Emerging Evidence Base for Adult Social Care Transformation: SCIE Research Briefing 31*. London: Social Care Institute for Excellence.

Needham, C. (2010) Commissioning for personalisation: from the fringes to the mainstream, *PMPA*, July.

Office for Disability Issues (2011) *Independent Living Strategy Brokerage and Support Planning*. http://odi.dwp.gov.uk/docs/ils/support-planning-and-brokerage-project-report.pdf

OPM (2010) *Delivering Personal Budgets for Adult Social Care: Reflections from Essex*. London: Office for Public Management.

Renata, S. (2010) The paradox of choice. Lecture for RSA 2010. http://www.thersa.org/events/video/archive/renata-salecl-the-paradox-of-choice (2 September 2011).

Richardson, L. (2005) User engagement in public services: policy and implementation. *Benefits* 13(3): 189–97.

Rummery, K. and Glendinning, C. (2000) Access to services as a civil and social right issue: the role of welfare professionals in regulating access to and commissioning services for disabled and older people under New Labour. *Social Policy and Administration*, 34(5): 529–50.

SCIE (2011) *People who Pay for Care: Quantitative and Qualitative Analysis of Self-funders in the Social Care Market*. http://www.thinklocalactpersonal.org.uk/_library/Resources/Personalisation/Localmilestones/People_who_pay_for_care_-_report_12_1_11_final.pdf (accessed 22 December 2011).

Small, N. (2000) User involvementL: selected review of the literature. In N. Small and P. Rhodes (eds) *Too Ill to Talk: User Involvement and Palliative Care*. London: Routledge.

Stevens, M., Glendinning, C., Jacobs, S., et al. (2011) Assessing the role of increasing choice in English social care services. *Journal of Social Policy*, 40: 257–74.

Williams, B. and Tyson, A. (2010) Self-direction, place and community: re-discovering the emotional depths: a conversation with social workers in a London borough. *Journal of Social Work Practice*. 24: 319–33.

7

Conclusion

Personalisation as a concept, ideology, philosophy and as a new way of social work practice is currently a hotly contested and debated reality. As this book has highlighted there is research that shows personalisation in a positive light and there is also research highlighting the difficulties with it. Personalisation also has mixed reactions from social workers, service users and carers. This book has sought to highlight some of the areas of consternation among social workers and carers while also seeking to highlight how personalisation can be immensely beneficial to service users in that it promises choice and control in a way that was never possible before.

Personalisation did not come about as a result of a Eureka moment but has emerged gradually as social consciousness of personhood grew. There has been a development in social and political thinking leading to the concept of consumer-citizen. Personalisation in that sense is a logical conclusion to the development of a particular way of thinking about people and especially about those who are vulnerable in society and require support. Personalisation says that if some one is vulnerable and in need of services it should not follow that they should be powerless and accept services in the way 'professionals' decide they should be provided. Personalisation focuses more on the ability of people rather than their disability believing that more often than not people needing services are quite capable of identifying how their needs can be met if they had the resources to do this.

At a philosophical and ideological level, few would have a problem with personalisation as it is all about being person centred and putting people first. It is about seeking to empower people and giving a voice to those in society who hitherto had no choice and control over significant areas of their lives. But part of the difficulties encountered within personalisation is due to a huge shift in roles of key players in adult social care, not least social workers (care managers) and commissioners. It takes time to reinvent one's role when there is a radically new way of providing social care. There is insecurity, doubt and suspicion regarding the motives for such radical change. The book has sought to identify where these emotions originate and to identify new and probably more relevant ways of 'doing social work' post personalisation.

Personalisation also brings to the fore the principles of social work and ethics and value base. Personalisation provides an opportunity for social work to re-discover itself and in many ways get back to the basics. It provides the opportunity to be person centred in approach and to engage with service users in an anti-oppressive way as more power is given to service users. Personalisation makes it necessary for the relationship between social worker and service user to be based on trust, self respect, responsibility and positive regard. In order to work, personalisation needs to be based on a relationship of co-production and partnership.

An area of major concern within personalisation is the issue of safeguarding. One of the major areas of opposition to personalisation is the possibility of abuse of vulnerable people. The concern is that if people who are vulnerable have money given to them it leaves them open to financial abuse. The chapter on safeguarding has dealt with issues of safeguarding putting it into context within personalisation. More responsibility always has more risk but positive risk taking leads to growth and often a more fulfilled life. So rather than clamp down on personalisation due to the possible risks it is important that the social worker seeks strategies to minimize risk of abuse.

The book has also discussed the perspective of service users and carers around personalisation and the impact it has had on their lives. There have been several very positive stories coming from service users and carers where personalisation has made a genuine difference to the quality of their lives. But there have also been some difficulties service users and carers have experienced with personalisation, as with the choice and control that personalisation provides it also brings greater responsibility. There has been some discussion on the development of brokerage services to help service users with the planning and implementation of their personal budget.

Finally, personalisation is such a radical change in social care that possibly future history of social care will consider pre-personalisation and post-personalisation social care. Therefore, it was important to conclude the book with a chapter on managing change and looking at the way ahead. The major change is the transformation from service user to consumer-citizen and the change in relationship between social worker and service users from provider recipient to co-production and partnership. This transformation in relationship brings with it its own opportunities and challenges. The chapter also discusses the important issues of development of the market in the post- personalisation scenario as choice will still be limited if the provider market for social care is under-developed.

The pedagogy of this book has been to try and engage and involve the reader in the debate and to encourage reflection on critical issues that have risen within the context of personalisation. The purpose of the book is to help identify and understand the issues presented by personalisation. It is not intended to be a polemic to convince the reader one way or the other but to present the issues as objectively as possible and allow the reader to come to their own conclusions about personalisation. However, it must be said that personalisation seems to be here to stay as it has the unanimous backing of all major political parties so the challenge is the make it work for service users. Awareness of the challenges presented in the book will hopefully set practitioners on the path to overcoming them and the opportunities presented will no doubt encourage towards embracing personalisation with and for service users.

Index

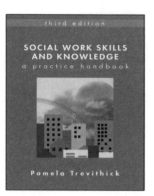

SOCIAL WORK SKILLS AND KNOWLEDGE
A Practice Handbook
Third Edition

Pamela Trevithick

9780335238071 (Paperback)
February 2012

eBook also available

Since its first publication in 2000, this best-selling text has been an invaluable resource for thousands of social workers preparing for life in practice. Written by an influential academic-practitioner, it is widely regarded as the leading book in its field.

Key features:

- 4 new chapters that integrate theory and practice in a Knowledge and Skills Framework
- 80 social work skills and interventions
- 12 appendices describing a range of different social work approaches

www.openup.co.uk